Chinatown Dreams

To Alyne—
Here's to dreams!
Geoffrey D.

To Alyne
Enjoy and Dream
big!
George Ow, Jr.
Temple Beth El

To Alyne:
Chinatown will live
forever!
Sandy Lydon
Feb 27, 2003
Soquel

To Alyne:
Dreams are special,
Keep them alive!
Tony Hill
Feb 27, 03

Chinatown

THE LIFE AND PHOTOGRAPHS

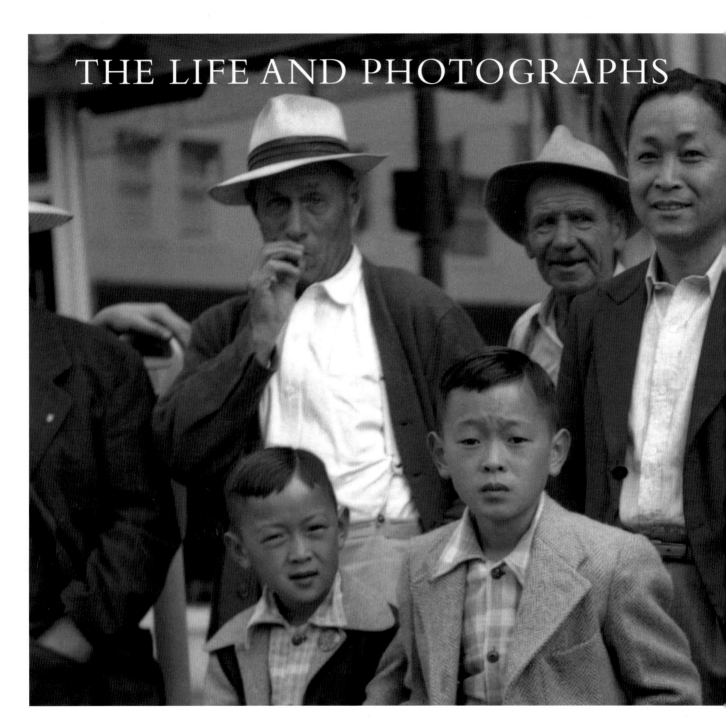

Dreams

OF GEORGE LEE

Geoffrey Dunn
EDITOR

Lisa Liu Grady

Tony Hill

James D. Houston

Sandy Lydon

Morton Marcus

George Ow, Jr.

Capitola Book Company
1601 41st Avenue, Capitola, CA 95010.
www.capitolabook.com

Photographs for this book have been provided by the Estate of George Lee
and Covello & Covello Photography. Walker Evans photo courtesy Library of Congress.

Book and cover designed by Mark Ong.

Dunn, Geoffrey (editor);
Grady, Lisa Liu; Hill, Tony;
Houston, James D.; Lydon, Sandy;
Marcus, Morton; Ow, Jr., George

Chinatown Dreams: The Life and Photographs of George Lee
1. George Lee (1922–1998)—biography. 2. George Lee (1922–1998)—photographs.
3. Chinese American history—Santa Cruz, California.
4. Documentary photography—United States. 5. Documentary photography—California.

Printed in China by C&C Offset, Ltd.

ISBN 0-932319-06-8
ISBN 0-932319-07-6 pbk.

10 09 08 07 06 05 04 03 02   6 5 4 3 2 1

What lies behind many versions of the [American] Dream

is the conception of America as a kind of magic environment

or society that has the power to transform people's lives,

the idea that the United States is not merely a new world,

but a different kind of world, a unique place

where the limitations, boundaries, and inequities

that formerly confined the human race

either do not exist or are about to disappear.

JAMES GUIMOND
American Photography and the American Dream

Contents

Introduction
1

Chinatown Dreams
The Life and Photographs of George Lee
GEOFFREY DUNN
3

The Immigrant's Lament
MORTON MARCUS
12

Santa Cruz Chinatown
15

Always on the Outside
Santa Cruz and Its Many Chinatowns
SANDY LYDON
39

I Remember Chinatown
GEORGE OW, JR.
43

World War II and Korea
55

East Side, West Side, All Around the Town
James D. Houston
71

Sharing an American Dream
Tony Hill
76

Community Portraits
79

She Stands
Lisa Liu Grady
85

Chinatown Farewell
91

The Photographer Remembers
Morton Marcus
95

Family Album
99

Captions and Commentary
on Selected Photographs
George Ow, Jr.
130

Contributors
139

Introduction

THIS BOOK BEGAN as a breakfast conversation among friends. Photographer George Lee, his nephew George Ow, Jr., Tony Hill, Sandy Lydon, Morton Marcus and I gradually developed the idea of featuring Lee's lifelong collection of photographs in an exhibit and accompanying book. In short order, the project grew to include writers James D. Houston and Lee's cousin-by-marriage Lisa Liu Grady, along with associate editors Buz Bezore and Madelyn McCaul. Mark Ong was called upon to serve as the book's designer, while Chris Lydon handled preliminary graphic work on the photographs. Cori Houston provided much-needed production assistance to help see the book through to completion.

George Lee was well into the time-consuming task of assembling his slides and making special prints

George Lee, Seaman Second Class, with Graflex, at naval photography school; Pensacola, Florida: 1943.

1

George Lee at Webber's Photo Shop: 1958.

for both the exhibition and the book when he was stricken with a massive stroke in the summer of 1998. He died shortly thereafter, surrounded by several generations of his extended family. The project went into a brief hiatus and then, after a prolonged period of grief, was resurrected with the loving assistance of Lee's widow, Priscilla, and his daughter, Patti.

In the fall of 2000, exhibit designers extraordinaire Charles Prentiss and Nikki Silva launched the first of several planned exhibits of Lee's work at the Museum of Art and History in Santa Cruz. The exhibit was one of the museum's most popular ever. This book now follows on the heels of that successful inaugural exhibit and in advance of what we hope will be several more to come. It is lovingly dedicated to Priscilla and Patti Lee, and to the memory of George Lee, whom we all miss dearly, but whose artistry and spirit live on in this book.

Geoffrey Dunn
Editor
Santa Cruz, California
November 2002

GEOFFREY DUNN

Chinatown Dreams
The Life and Photographs of George Lee

THE PHOTOGRAPHS OF George Lee constitute one of the most important collections of documentary images in the California archive. Taken over a period of more than 60 years, Lee's artistically rendered portraits and landscapes chronicle a significant era and experience in California history. The son of Chinese immigrants, Lee constructed an inside—and profoundly intimate—view of a California Chinese American community, one that would ultimately span five generations by the time of his death in the summer of 1998.[1]

George Lee lived and breathed photography. He was a consummate professional and a highly trained artist. He began his formal training in photography as a teenager and he would continue to earn a living in his beloved trade for six decades. He identified so closely with the profession that in literally hundreds of

3

self-portraits and casual family snapshots, he is holding some form of photographic equipment, most often a camera. Four years after his death, it is all but impossible to think of him as separate from his craft. His brother-in-law, George Ow, Sr., who arrived in Santa Cruz from China as a teenager in the 1930s and who was immediately befriended by Lee, noted that "George must have been born with a camera in his hand. That's just *who he was.*"

In addition to being a widely celebrated, award-winning documentary photographer, Lee was also a photo news journalist for local newspapers and the Associated Press, and a commercial photographer for several other regional publications.[2] He won numerous awards for photographic equipment displays and taught photography at the collegiate level to several generations of students on the Central California coast.[3]

While George Lee's life and artistic vision sprang from a California Chinatown—a vision that has both shaped and inspired this book—it should be duly noted that Lee's artistry transcended the Chinatown of his youth and early adulthood. The more than 100 photographs collected for this book reflect just a small sampling of his photographic oeuvre. He took landscape photographs of the Sierra Nevada, for instance, that rival those of Ansel Adams. He took travel photos on his journeys around the world that were suitable for publication in *National Geographic*. He documented the Miss California Pageant in Santa Cruz for decades and recorded floods and earthquakes and building demolitions. He also took thousands of

George Lee with Rolleicord: Circa 1941.

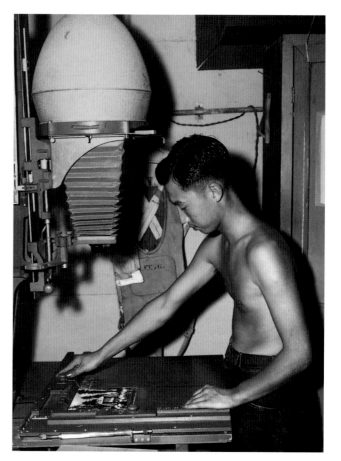

George Lee with photo enlarger,
during Navy years in the South Pacific: Circa 1944.

Yee Hen Bok preparing lunch: 1941.

George Lee taking pictures on a ladder:
Later 1940s, after World War II. Photo by Ed Webber.

Kodachrome "snapshots" that would fit comfortably into family scrapbooks across America.

The photographs collected in this book were chosen for their historic and artistic value, of course, but also because of the way in which they reflect the artist himself. For the most part, they chronicle Lee's life—and the lives of his extended family—from the 1930s through the 1980s. They reflect his dreams and aspirations, and they capture the spirit of those who loved and knew him best. Indeed, if there were one thing in George Lee's life that rivaled photography, it was his family—so much so that the two are inexorably linked in his photographs.

Modest and understated, perhaps to a fault, Lee was nevertheless proud of his photographic archive and fully recognized its significance. He kept extensive files of more than 3,000 prints and negatives, which were generally organized around themes and chronologies that have provided structure and direc-tion to this book. His archive represents a unique and fascinating chronicle for much of the twentieth cen-tury—and he intended it as such.

George Lee was born in San Francisco, California, on December 19, 1922. As a young boy, he also was known by the Chinese nickname of *Go,* Can-tonese for "the tall one." His father, Sung Si Lee, a native of Canton, China, had come to America some time around the turn of the century as a so-called paper merchant, which allowed him entry into Cali-fornia during a period of profoundly limited Chinese immigration. His mother, Gue Shee Lee, who was born in a southern Chinese village, Hong San, near Macao in 1900, had arrived in San Francisco in the immediate aftermath of World War I. She was nearly two decades younger than her husband.

When Lee was three years old, the family relocated briefly to Tracy, in the sweltering San Joaquin Valley,

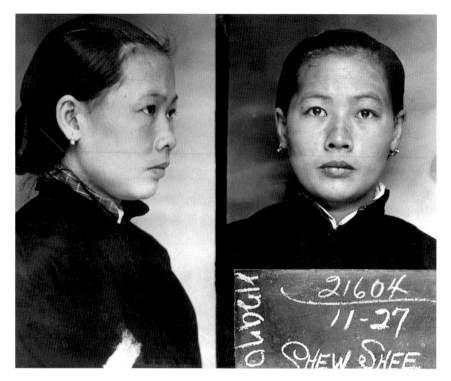

TOP LEFT: Sung Si Lee, father of George Lee, immigration photo: 1903.

TOP RIGHT: Gue Shee Lee, mother of George Lee, immigration photo: 1922.

BOTTOM RIGHT: Sung Si Lee, immigration photo: 1922.

then to the coastal fishing and farming community of Santa Cruz, situated on the north end of Monterey Bay. His father took a job as a cook at the Wilder Dairy Ranch, on the Coastal Road north of the city, working six days a week on the ranch, then returning by train to the family home for Sunday dinners. The family eventually grew to seven children. George was followed by Emily, Rose, Wee, Young, Luella and Jun.

The Lee family lived in what was the fourth of Santa Cruz's Chinatown communities, commonly referred to as Birkenseer's Chinatown, on Bellevue Place.[4] Nestled between the San Lorenzo River and Santa Cruz's downtown business district, the Santa Cruz Chinatown of Lee's childhood and adolescence was one marginalized from Santa Cruz's northern European mainstream. It was also bordered on the north by the landmark Hotel Garibaldi, a colorful rooming house, saloon and restaurant frequented by working-class Italian immigrants of the region. Later in his life Lee observed that "most of my childhood friends were Italians."

Indeed, it was one such childhood friend, Frank Del Bianco, who introduced him to photography as a young teenager. "He was the smart one," Lee would later quip. "He went into banking."

The first photographic images in Lee's life were family portraits and those attached to the immigration documents of his mother and father. He and his family were also photographed by Lee's elementary school teacher, Alice Halsey, in the early 1930s. These

6

TOP LEFT: Stock certificate signifying fifty shares of Lee Family Association stock owned by Sung Si Lee: Circa 1890s.

TOP MIDDLE: Wee Lee registration to Lee Family Association in San Francisco: 1929.

TOP RIGHT: Gue Shee Lee with George Lee at one year of age: 1923.

BOTTOM LEFT: Gue Shee Lee holding baby Young and Wee. Santa Cruz Chinatown: 1931. Photo by Alice Halsey.

BOTTOM RIGHT: Gue Shee Lee with her children (left to right) Rose, Wee, baby Young, George and Emily. Santa Cruz Chinatown: 1931. Photo by Alice Halsey.

rare photographic images assumed a special place in the visual texture of Lee's early childhood. He took special care to preserve them throughout his life.

Lee was educated in local schools—Laurel Elementary and Mission Hill Junior High—before entering Santa Cruz High School in the fall of 1936. He had already developed a reputation as a solid photographer by then, working after school and during the summer for the Camera Shop, an early photography business on Walnut Avenue. After graduating from high school in January of 1941, Lee continued his studies—including photography—at the nearby junior college in Salinas.

American photography had experienced a major renaissance during the 1930s with the formation of the Federal Photography Division of the Resettlement Administration, later to become the Farm Security Administration (FSA), under the direction of Roy Emerson Stryker. Photographers such as Walker Evans, Dorothea Lange, Arthur Rothstein and John Vachon were all hired by Stryker during the height of the Depression, and their photographs came to dominate the visual landscape of the nation for the better part of a decade.[5]

The teenage Lee was clearly influenced by these photographers. In an interview I conducted with him in the 1980s, Lee noted that the images of the FSA photographers, along with those of Edward Steichen, Ansel Adams and Edward Weston, who was taking photos in nearby Point Lobos at the time, had indeed had an impact on him.

Unlike the FSA photographers, however, who traveled around the country in search of poverty, or what anthropologists call "the other," Lee photographed his own community in Santa Cruz's Chinatown. The men—named Chin Lai, Lee Lam Bok, Yee Hen Bok, Ah Fook, and Moon Lai Bok—were the last of a generation that had come at the end of the nineteenth century to *Gum Shan,* as they called it, the "Land of Gold Mountain," working in the fields and laundries and gambling halls of the Central California coast.

Bud Fields, Hale County, Alabama: 1936.
Photo by Walker Evans.

They had come from China with dreams and aspirations for a better life, but had found instead an institutionalized racism that relegated them to the periphery of mainstream American society.

Lee, who had recently saved up enough money to purchase a high-grade, German-made Rolleicord camera, knew and loved the men whom he photographed. Indeed, they were a part of the very fabric of his life. Many years later, Lee told me that he viewed the aging men as "natural subject matter" for his burgeoning interest in photography. "They probably wouldn't let anybody else take pictures of them."

In certain respects Lee's classic portraits of the men who were "longtime Californ'" echo those of the FSA photographers. The lines on these aged men's faces flow into the weathered wood grains of the clapboard redwood buildings of the Santa Cruz Chinatown. There is an artistry to them strikingly reminiscent of Evans's facial portraits of the Burroughs, Fields and Tengle families in Hale County, Alabama, that appeared with James Agee's prose in the legendary *Let Us Now Praise Famous Men.*

Take, for instance, Lee's photo of Lee Lam Bok, and compare it with Evans's portrait of Bud Fields (see photo above). The framing, lighting and backdrop of the two images are remarkably similar.

Lee Lam Bok: 1941.

The defining difference, of course, is the absence of distance between Lee and his subjects. The elderly men in Lee's portraits are neither portrayed as "the other" nor as exotic. Nor are they victimized as poster children for poverty, as were the subjects of many FSA photographs, most notably those of Evans and Lange. They are humanized—rendered as equals among the photographer, subject and audience. We are not asked to take pity on them; we are asked to encounter them as individual human beings.

This was no accident. Like Toyo Miyatake, a Japanese American photographer who is best known for having smuggled a lens and film into the Manzanar concentration camp during World War II, Lee was chronicling a community of which he was a part. He was an insider looking in. While Lee's images lack some of the dramatic elements and artistic framing of

Lange's and Evans's more celebrated photographs, in a very real sense they are more immediate and more accurate as documentary images. There is a complexity to Lee's documentary construction of a human life shamefully absent in many of the FSA photos.[6]

At the age of 20, Lee enlisted in the U.S. Navy, where he served as a military photographer throughout World War II and, later, in the Korean War.[7] He undertook formal photography training in Pensacola, Florida, and was then sent to several combat zones in the Pacific theater.

As it did for many men of his generation, World War II provided a defining moment in Lee's life. Lee's documentary photos from this era—Tonkinese women selling grass skirts; fishermen and their canoes in the New Hebrides; American sailors celebrating VJ Day—are taken from the perspective of an enlisted man. There is an ease and egalitarian quality to his images noticeably lacking in both the formal government photographs and the journalistic images of the times.

Following the war, Lee returned home to Santa Cruz and immediately went to work in the business of photography. His wartime buddy Eddy Webber started a camera business in downtown Santa Cruz and Lee became a fixture there for the next 40 years. George Ow, Jr., points out that his uncle was "one of the first Chinese Americans in Santa Cruz to be hired to work 'up front' in a retail store not owned by a Chinese."

In June of 1949, Lee married his longtime sweetheart, Priscilla Wong, who had immigrated to the United States from Canton, China, in 1940. The Lee family and Priscilla's father had been friends in the Santa Cruz Chinatown during the Depression, and George and Priscilla's courtship became formal once George returned to Santa Cruz from the war.

Lee's photographs began appearing regularly in the *Santa Cruz Sentinel* upon his return to Santa Cruz, and some, like a Chinese New Year photo of his

daughter, Patti, were picked up by the Associated Press. He took literally *thousands* of family photographs during the next four decades.

Lee also became a beloved teacher of photography throughout the region. He taught hundreds of local

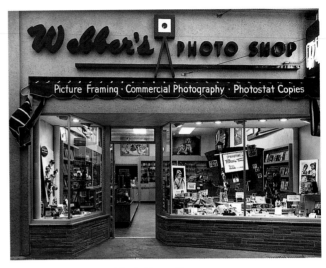

Webber's Photo Shop: 1950s.

George Lee's press pass.

Patti Lee with firecrackers: 1958.

students at Cabrillo College, Harbor High, and Santa Cruz Adult School, and was instrumental in bringing darkrooms to Harbor High and Mission Hill Junior High School. He took courses and kept up with innovations in the profession until he died.

During the 1980s, with the publication of Sandy Lydon's seminal work, *Chinese Gold: The Chinese in the Monterey Bay Region,* Lee was inspired to pull out his old prints and negatives for inclusion in Lydon's book, a subsequent museum exhibit and a documentary film.[8] "I knew back then that my photos would be of historical value," he told me shortly before he died. "I knew they were worth saving. I just didn't know it would all fly by so quickly."[9]

1 Earlier versions of this chapter appeared as "He Captured Their Lives for Posterity: The Way Things Were," *The News (Santa Cruz County),* October 23, 1986; and "Chinatown Dreams: The Life and Photographs of George Lee," *Metro Santa Cruz,* October 18, 2000, both by Geoffrey Dunn. Formal interviews with George Lee were conducted by the author in the fall of 1986 and spring of 1997, and informal discussions took place throughout decades of friendship. This chapter also draws upon interviews conducted with George Lee's siblings, including Luella Lee Churchill and Jun Lee; his brother-in-law, George Ow, Sr.; his nephew, George Ow, Jr.; and an unpublished essay by his niece, Karin Naomi Yien. See also Wallace Baine, "Gold Mountain," *Santa Cruz Sentinel,* October 8, 2000, pp. B1 and B3.

2 Lee's most widely published photo, of his three-year-old daughter, Patti, holding firecrackers, was issued during the Chinese New Year by the Associated Press on February 20, 1958.

3 An article entitled "These Windows Mean Business," focusing on Lee's award-winning window displays, appeared in *Photo Dealer,* July 1960.

4 For a comprehensive description of Chinese American history in the region, see Sandy Lydon, *Chinese Gold: The Chinese in the Monterey Bay Region* (Capitola Book Company: 1985); and Geoffrey Dunn, "Climbing Golden Mountain," *Santa Cruz Is in the Heart* (Capitola Book Company: 1989), pp. 17-32. For a more detailed account of the Ow and Lee families, see Dunn, "Atop the Golden Mountain," ibid, pp. 67-85.

5 For accounts of the FSA photographers, see James Guimond, *American Photography and the American Dream* (Chapel Hill: 1991); Therese Thau Heyman, *Celebrating a Collection: The Works of Dorothea Lange* (Oakland Museum: 1978); F. Jack Hurley, *Portrait of a Decade: Roy Stryker and the Development of Documentary Photography in the Thirties* (Louisiana: 1972); F. Jack Hurley, *Russell Lee, Photographer* (Morgan & Morgan: 1978); Sandra Phillips, *Dorothea Lange: American Photographs* (Chronicle Books: 1994); and Roy Emerson Stryker and Nancy Wood, *In This Proud Land* (Rapoport: 1973).

6 For critical reflections on the FSA photographers, see Geoffrey Dunn, "Photographic License," *Metro,* January 19, 1995, pp. 20-24; Vicki Goldberg, "Looking at the Poor in a Gilded Frame," *The New York Times,* April 9, 1995; and James Curtis, *Mind's Eye, Mind's Truth: FSA Photography Reconsidered* (Temple: 1989).

7 An undated news clip from the *Santa Cruz Riptide* of 1942, headlined "Local Chinese Youth in Navy: Seaman George Lee," notes that Lee was "studying engineering and photography [at] Salinas Junior [C]ollege until last December when he determined to get into the Big Show." It also noted that "the young Chinese graduated from Santa Cruz high school, where he displayed marked talent for photography" and that in "his spare time and during the summer months he was employed at the Camera Shop where he did some excellent photography." The *Service Cardinal,* published in 1948 by Santa Cruz High School to honor those alumni who served in the armed forces during World War II, contains a detailed record of Lee's first stint in the Navy (p. 239): "George entered the service on December 12, 1942, and received his boot training at Farragut, Idaho; Photography School, Pensacola, Florida; Photo-Lithography School, Anacostia, D.C.; operational training, North Island, San Diego, California [and] Arcata, California. From February 12, 1944 to June 2, 1945, he was in Ford Island, Honolulu, Espiritu Santos, New Hebrides; Pitylu Island; and Admiralty Islands. George received a Letter of Commendation from Admiral Royal Commander of Task Group 79.2 while stationed in the Admiralty Islands for photo work done in New Guinea. He returned to the States on June 29, 1945. After his leave, he was stationed in Shelton, Washington, and USN Air Station, Sandpoint, Washington, and was discharged November, 12, 1540, at Bremerton, Washington."

8 The documentary film *Chinese Gold: The Chinese in the Monterey Bay Region* (45 minutes) was produced by Geoffrey Dunn and Mark Schwartz (1986) and based on the book by Sandy Lydon. It is available for distribution through the Capitola Book Company (www.capitola-book.com). The initial posthumous exhibit of Lee's work was held at the Santa Cruz Museum of Art and History from September 23, 2000, through January 21, 2001.

9 A lengthy obituary honoring Lee's life and his work appeared in the *Santa Cruz Sentinel,* July 23, 1998, p. A8.

MORTON MARCUS

The Immigrant's Lament

If I am old now
I feel no different
than when I was young
and new in this place
and thought I was a chunk
of my homeland
broken off and exported
for a foreigner's
profit or pleasure—
the body of a teapot
with a soul of silk.

It was more, much more
than being a stranger here.
It was as if I had been ripped
from the earth in a flood,
carried by restless seas,
and thrown on the shores
of this distant land
like some gasping creature
you stared at
more in bewilderment
than disbelief.

Your stares nudged me
like a boot determining
if I was real, or you laughed
at my looks and clothes
and different ways,
thinking they gave you
the right to order me about
for your most menial tasks,
and to teach me how
to pray and think and do
everything just like you.

Now I want to be buried
in my homeland,
interred with the dust
of my ancestors, a dust
I'll wear like a silk robe,
for the pain of separation
I've carried clenched
inside me all these years
will unroll like a bolt
of the finest cloth and I'll
wrap myself in it like a cocoon.

You with your foreign eyes,
what do you know
about the world that goes on
behind this face
so impassively turned
toward you? My heart
breaks into pieces
as easily as that dish
you so casually place
on your dining room table
and call china.

Santa Cruz Chinatown

Santa Cruz Chinatown: Early 1940s.

Ah Fook: 1941.

17

CHINATOWN DREAMS

Yee Hen Bok cutting tofu that the old men made for themselves: 1941.

Mook Lai Bok smoking pipe: 1941.

Chinatown houses: 1941.

CHINATOWN DREAMS

Yee Hen Bok: 1941.

Moon Lai Bok hanging laundry at Chee Kong Tong Temple: 1941.

CHINATOWN DREAMS

Yee Hen Bok smoking self-rolled Bull Durham cigarette: 1941.

San Lorenzo River, looking from Soquel Bridge to present County Building and San Lorenzo Park: 1941.

CHINATOWN DREAMS

Ah Fook and George Ow, Jr.: 1948.

CHINATOWN DREAMS

Last occupied building in Chinatown; Allan Liu and Jun Lee
playing near George Lee's Western Flyer bicycle: 1941.

Georgina Wong and George Ow, Jr.: Chinatown, 1947.

CHINATOWN DREAMS

Gue Shee Lee harvesting corn beside San Lorenzo River with grandchildren
George Ow, Jr., and David Lee Ow: 1949.

Chee Kong Tong Temple with Donny Liu, Allan Liu and Jun Lee playing army among the Chinese mustard plants. The Hotel Garibaldi is to the right: 1941.

Gue Shee Lee
on China Lane: 1941.

Rose Lee and Kim Wong: 1941.

Emily Lee Ow and George Ow, Jr.: 1943.   Emily Lee Ow and George Ow, Jr.: 1944.

George Ow, Jr., reading the *Service Cardinal:* 1950.

George Ow, Jr., atop car: 1948.

George Ow, Jr., and David Lee Ow: 1951.

Ronald and Linda Wong in front of grandmother
Gue Shee Lee's chicken coop: 1954

Young Lee, Chinatown: 1943.

#30 China Lane, formerly Bellevue Place: 1941

36

George Ow with his Hupmobile: 1941.

Chinatown sunset looking toward old town clock and flag flying on top of old county jail: 1941.

CHINATOWN DREAMS

Always on the Outside

Santa Cruz and Its Many Chinatowns

APPARITIONS emerging
and then dissolving in the mists on the far edges of
mainstream culture, the Chinese are an integral part of
California's historical landscape. Vague, indistinct,
nameless, until recently no one noticed that they were
the simple answer to many of the state's basic historical questions: Who built the railroads? Who started the
commercial fishing industry? Who cleaned the rooms
in all those hotels? Who cooked the food for all the
lumbermen? Who helped diversify California's agri-
culture?

Quietly and anonymously, Chinese muscle built
California.

Chinatowns sprouted wherever Chinese sweat and
blood mingled with stone and sand and soil. At first,
temporary China Camps sprouted in the Sierra
Nevada goldfields and fishing villages along the coast.
Then Chinese tents marched beside the rails that

39

stitched California together. As California became more permanent, so did the Chinatowns. False-front wooden buildings, laundries and boardinghouses replaced the tents. Soon, every place, it seemed, had a Chinatown.

For those Chinese who ventured from the Middle Kingdom to the world's far corners, Chinatowns were the vessels within which they carried their truths, their dreams and their hopes. Behind Chinatown walls, they could preserve and protect their culture, which stretched back to the beginnings of recorded time.

Convinced that theirs was the most developed civilization on Earth (and finding few contradictions), the Chinese rarely left the Middle Kingdom. But when they did so during a period of tremendous emigration in the 1800s, they dotted the world with tiny microcosms of the home they left behind. From Bangkok, Djakarta, Manila, Yokohama, Calcutta and Tahiti to London, Amsterdam, Mexico City, Havana, New York City and San Francisco, every place had its Chinese city-within-a-city.

For most non-Chinese, Chinatown was an exotic place whose walls concealed the forbidden and the unknowable. Beginning with lurid nineteenth-century accounts and fueled by later pulp fiction and film, the image of Chinatown was forever welded to the popular mental landscape as that "other" world, a sensual enclave indecipherable to outsiders.

This image was based, in part, on an element of truth: most Chinatowns provided recreational activities for Chinese men far from home. The three dominant industries were gambling, opium and prostitution. Controlled and operated by the Chinese themselves, these businesses gave a certain tone to Chinatown, and when non-Chinese found themselves welcomed as clients, the image was forever fixed in the mainstream imagination: Chinatown was an exciting mixture of pleasure and danger. This popular notion said much more about the observers than the Chinese who lived there, of course, and the walls of Chinatown became mirrors reflecting back the taboo fantasies of those on the outside.

For gregarious, family-centered Chinese immigrants, Chinatown was a comforting womb whose sounds, smells and tastes harkened of home. Chinatown was a refuge from the cacophony of the wider community, a retreat for the heart and spirit, a sanctuary in which to relax and dream.

Cultural confidence attracted the Chinese to each other, but the wind-whipped fires of racism and discrimination hardened the walls of Chinatown into a tough shell. Physically and culturally distinct, Chinese immigrants often were the scapegoats for whatever ills plagued the host culture. Economic slumps, unemployment, droughts and even earthquakes were blamed on the Chinese. Chinatowns served as both cultural repositories and fortresses against the torch-bearing mob.

It was extremely difficult for the Chinese to put down permanent roots in California. Federal law forbade their becoming naturalized citizens, and immigration restrictions made it all but impossible to go back to China and then return. They could not vote, marry Caucasians or (after 1913) own real property in California. The Geary Act of 1892 required the Chinese to carry identification cards at all times. They were forbidden to use carrying poles on public streets, and even the flying of kites was made illegal in one coastal city. They lived under more legal restrictions than any immigrant group in California history.

Bound and trussed by laws restricting their cultural practices, the Chinese retreated still further into their Chinatowns.

Each of the Monterey Bay Area's four largest Chinatowns was unique to its location. Monterey's Chinatown was anchored by the fishing industry, while Salinas and Watsonville had Chinatowns that were primarily service communities to the hundreds of farm laborers who drove the Central Coast's agricultural engine.

Santa Cruz's Chinatown was the region's smallest, and its history reflects the tenuous relationship that the Chinese had with the seaside town.

Santa Cruz's nineteenth-century economy was dominated by the manufacture of lumber, lime and leather products—industries in which the Chinese were allowed but a token role. Santa Cruz was also home to some of the leaders of the state's anti-Chinese movement. Ever vulnerable, Santa Cruz's Chinatown always existed on the periphery, skittering around the edges of the dominant community until it eventually had five separate locations.

Santa Cruz's first Chinatown emerged in 1862 when the California Powder Works built a huge blasting and gunpowder plant two miles up the San Lorenzo River. Chinese laborers leveled ground, built walls and drilled a huge tunnel through which the river was diverted to drive the factory's equipment.

After the plant was completed, many of the men stayed to work in the company's cooperage, making barrels for the powder. A small Chinatown sprang up at the factory and a second emerged on Willow Street in Santa Cruz. Following the wholesale dismissal of all the company's Chinese employees in 1878, the two consolidated along the river on Front Street, remaining until 1894.

Compared with the other Chinatowns in the region, Santa Cruz's version was small. Most of the forty or so people living near Front Street were involved with the laundries located along the river. An equal number of Chinese men lived scattered throughout Santa Cruz, employed as cooks, domestics and market gardeners. There was but one Chinese woman listed as living in the entire town in 1880.

Rents in Chinatown were cheap because the low-lying lots were exposed to flooding each winter. The front of each narrow, two-story building sat at street level, while its rear perched on pilings over the river bottom behind. In most years, there was enough clearance beneath the buildings to accommodate high water, but the winter floods periodically would force the Chinese inhabitants to move their belongings to the second story.

Nineteenth-century Santa Cruz was a difficult place for Chinese immigrants to live, not only because they had to contend with myriad restrictions imposed by the state and federal governments, but also because they lived in constant fear of an increasingly hostile populace. Since they did not play a major role in the town's economy, the Chinese became the targets of periodic anti-Chinese hostility which swept through the community. Santa Cruz was the regional anti-Chinese epicenter, and the small Chinese community's perch on the riverbank was constantly threatened by abatement and even mob violence.

Fire, always a fear in every Chinatown, finally became a reality in April 1894, when all of the Front Street Chinatown burned down, along with much of Santa Cruz's northern business district. At that point, the small Chinese community split in two. Some members moved to George Birkenseer's river-bottom property behind Front Street, while the remainder moved over to a small Chinatown on the opposite side of town.

The two Chinatowns rejoined in 1905 along the San Lorenzo River, and the Chinese men built the last Chee Kong Tong hall on the water's edge. Founded originally as a patriotic society pledged to overthrow the Manchu government in the old country, the Chee Kong Tong evolved into a multifaceted organization in Chinese California. Religious organization, convalescent home, political action committee and benevolent society, the Chee Kong Tong served as surrogate family for the predominantly male Chinese community.

Accounts of daily life in Santa Cruz's nineteenth-century Chinatown are extremely rare. An 1894 legal proceeding provides one clear glimpse. A merchant named Ham Tung attempted to return to the United States after a visit to China. Since merchants were exempt from the return prohibitions, it was up to Ham Tung to prove that he had, indeed, lived in Santa Cruz. During the cross-examination by government officials, Ham Tung described a narrow world in which he rarely ventured beyond Chinatown's friendly embrace. He knew little of the town surrounding his home, and when asked to name the town's primary business street a block west of Chinatown, Ham Tung remembered Pacific Avenue only as "the white man's street." Unable to give answers sufficiently detailed to satisfy the government, Ham Tung was deported to China.

The best views of Santa Cruz's early Chinatowns come from the pen of a remarkable newspaper reporter named Ernest Otto. Born in Santa Cruz in 1871, Otto grew up in the days when little boys were free to roam everywhere. Since local Chinese children were so rare, the Chinese were tolerant of the white boys who ventured into Chinatown on a regular basis. Otto was one of them. He began writing for the local newspapers in the early 1880s, and many of his articles and columns chronicled the special and daily events in Chinatown. Otto's fair and objective writings acted as a balance to the dominant anti-Chinese line taken by the town's civic leadership.

Otto's columns bring Santa Cruz Chinatown to life: the smells of sandalwood and incense, the sounds of the three-piece band playing on festive occasions, the crackle of firecrackers set off during the Lunar New Year, the early morning call of the Chinese market gardeners hawking their wares along the city streets. Most importantly, while others in Santa Cruz wrote of the "heathen Chinese," Otto described them differently. "No one could ever forget those kindly China boys," he wrote toward the end of his career. "No matter how old they were, they were always China boys."

And "China boys" was apt, since the community was almost all male. Otto notes that throughout its long history in Santa Cruz, Chinatown had so few female residents that, years later, he could easily name them without hesitation. All were the wives of Chinese merchants.

The census of 1920 corroborates Otto's analysis. Twenty-two of the 29 Chinese residents were single men, their average age being 52 years. The only females were members of the Chin and Lam families. Those two women and three female children were the only exceptions to the all-male community; and the only American citizens in the community were four America-born children. The effects of immigration restrictions imposed between 1882 and 1920 were dramatically highlighted in these Santa Cruz Chinatown numbers.

The river may have been the bottom rung of Santa Cruz's political and economic hierarchy, but it was a wondrous place to grow up. With the tules and willows as their playground, the first America-born generation of Santa Cruz Chinese grew up in a multicultural neighborhood that included African Americans, Italians and Chinese.

Floods continued to whittle away at the community in the riverbed, with the flood of 1940 being notable for the second-story rescue of several residents of the Chee Kong Tong building. The centrifugal forces of education and opportunity also dispersed the second generation until the Christmastime flood in December 1955 and subsequent redevelopment finally pushed Santa Cruz's last Chinatown into extinction.

Most of California's old Chinatowns met a similar fate as the postwar forces of downtown redevelopment and revitalization swept through the state. The Army Corps of Engineers built a phalanx of levees to contain the San Lorenzo River, and Chinatown was covered over with asphalt and shopping centers—and the future.

What is most amazing about the story of the Chinese in Santa Cruz is that there are *any* Chinese connected to the old Birkenseer Chinatown still living in the seaside community. No regional Chinese community was more restricted and harassed than the one in Santa Cruz. Yet, like the vegetation that often bursts forth following a forest fire, the America-born generation exploded out of the river bottom and achieved successes far beyond anything that could have been imagined by those pioneer Chinese who first arrived here in 1862.

I Remember Chinatown

THIS IS THE STORY OF the Chinatown I remember, the Chinatown in which I was raised, and it is the story behind the photographs in this book, photographs that George Lee took through the years. The people I knew as a boy are wonderfully alive for me in Uncle George's photos, and I don't want you to think of this book as a roll call of the dead. I'd rather you look at it as the naming of those who were alive here in another time, those who were an integral part of building the community we now share, so that they—and what they accomplished—will not be forgotten.

I am 59 years old, almost past middle age. These days, I often stroll where Chinatown used to be. The old brick Hall of Records, a downtown Santa Cruz landmark since it was built in 1882, is now the gift shop of the Museum of Art and History, which itself is

Wee, Emily, and Rose Lee on Pacific Avenue in front of Woolworth's Building,
Santa Cruz: 1931. Photo by Alice Halsey.

housed in the old jail building. Across the street was my Chinatown, starting where Hobee's Restaurant now sits and leading past the Riverfront Theater to the banks of the San Lorenzo River. The walking path between the two Galleria buildings is where China Lane ran. My grandmother's house stood between today's restaurant and theater, close to a bronze plaque that proclaims a Chinatown once flourished here.

Most people who visit or work in this shopping-office complex don't know that it occupies the site of a former Chinatown. Some members of my own family don't know it. Perhaps future generations of the family won't know that they have Chinese ancestry. But George Lee's photographs bring it all back. Uncle George, Uncle Hong and my father, George Ow, Sr., are still aglow with youthful vigor in these post–World War II photos—returning young lions in a new America being cleansed of old anti-Chinese laws.

The old men who had laid the groundwork for my uncles, my father, me and my children are still vibrantly alive. In Uncle George's pictures, my mother and

Auntie Ro are young again, loving mothers brimming with energy. You can see Uncle Young as a teenager, proud of the salmon and halibut he caught to help feed our large, always-hungry clan. There's even Uncle Wee in his *pachuco* haircut before he went off to fight in the Korean War. And, look: Georgina Wong and I are eating apples and riding our tricycles.

It All Seems Like Only Yesterday

Sunday dinner.

It must be 1946 or 1947. I am four years old. World War II has ended, and Uncle George has just gotten out of the Navy. I know from constant family talk that he took pictures from airplanes, flying over enemy ships and Japanese-held islands. I also know that since my father was prone to seasickness, he and his cousin, Uncle Hong, had joined the Army.

But these tidbits of family lore are of no concern to me at the moment because Uncle George and my father are chasing me. I am sure that I can outrun them, can lead them on a merry obstacle course through all of my favorite play areas. Giggling all the while, I sprint down the hill with the pink climbing rose bush, past the chicken coop, through Grandma's garden, down to the river's edge.

But I have misjudged these grown men who have suddenly appeared in my life from a place called war. They have been given the task of bringing me home so that everyone can start Sunday dinner, and their long legs catch up with me before I can even reach the slope that leads to the garden. I am amazed at how powerful and quick they are. They snatch me up with their strong hands, raise me high overhead and carry me into the kitchen to join the rest of the family for Sunday dinner.

The entire inside of the wooden house is made of redwood slats painted with a satiny fern-green enamel. Exposed pipes run the length of the walls and bare light bulbs hang on black wires from the ceiling.

George Lee with F-56 Aerial Camera, Shelton, Washington: 1945.

The dangling light in the kitchen spreads a pale yellow glow on the family eating and talking below.

The kitchen is alive with relatives this day, as it is every Sunday. Mom and Dad have driven up from their new grocery store in Monterey, and aunts and uncles who left Chinatown, now that Chinese can live in other areas, are happy to be reunited—if only temporarily—with the rest of the family.

There is so much food. Chinese-style boiled and fried chicken from grandma's chicken coop. Mounds of rice and mashed potatoes served on large gray ceramic dishes decorated with blue fish. Corn, peas, string beans, bok choy, carrots, radishes—everything just picked from the garden—piled high on white platters emblazoned with vermilion dragons and phoenixes. Beautiful salmon and ling cod caught by Uncle Wee and Uncle Young share space with American dishes, with Chinese dishes.

We have more than enough to eat, but we never forget that our relatives in China are going hungry, some starving to death. In America, however, even poor Chinese immigrants can have a table loaded with food. We are so lucky.

My maternal grandmother, called *Poa* in Chinese, reigns during Sunday dinner. Just after the war, she is in her forties, short, stocky, energetic, confident and brash. As the mother of seven, she has to be. She knows a little English, and that—plus her forceful character—makes her a leader in our little Chinatown. She immigrated during the 1920s, one of the few Chinese women to make it through the harrowing ocean voyage, maze of anti-Chinese laws and grueling interrogation at the embarkation center on San Francisco's Angel Island.

By using a common ruse of the time, Poa was able to circumvent American laws created to eliminate or hinder Chinese immigration. Since the only Chinese women allowed into the United States were wives of merchants, Poa's husband and my grandfather, impoverished cook Sung Si Lee, did what countless other Chinese seeking immigration for their spouses did: he paid a relative to list him as a business partner. So, through an ironic series of circumstances, a country intending to exclude my grandmother and her children from social and economic advancement had turned a poor peasant from China into a merchant's wife in America.

Poa is above all, though, a wife and mother. When chickens are needed for dinner, she goes down to her coop, picks out a few and dispatches them herself with a cleaver. She uses every part of the chicken: blood is added to soup, the feet reserved as a tasty delicacy for respected family elders, and the feathers mixed with vinegar and other ingredients as an antidote for my cases of poison oak. Poison oak is terribly itchy, and spreading warm, smelly, wet chicken feathers on it is a torture that always ends in screaming and crying.

Times are good now and we can cook two or three chickens for a Sunday dinner, if we want. Before the war, things weren't as good. A Sunday chicken dinner then consisted of one bird divided among nine people and laid atop partially filled bowls of rice. "You are so lucky, Junior," my Auntie Lu says. "Back then, the girls had last pick and I would only get the small part of a wing. Your mom learned to like what goes over the fence last." But now we eat all the chicken, rice and mashed potatoes we can fit into our stomachs. My dad says that I was born at the right time, "under a lucky star."

George Lee is the most striking person at Sunday dinner. He is very slender and the tallest man in Chinatown. His Chinese name is *Go,* which means "tall." The Navy gave him muscles and all the food he could eat. He has a ready smile and looks people directly in the eye when he talks. Besides having been an honor student at Santa Cruz High School and flying all over the South Pacific for the Navy, Uncle George studied at Salinas College (now Hartnell) for a year and is the first member of the family to receive any kind of higher education. He is "no dummy," as he likes to say.

In addition to breaking new ground for both his family and the Chinese community, Uncle George is as generous as he is smart. When still a boy, his best friend was Frankie Del Bianco. Frankie dreamed of becoming an Air Force pilot, but failed to take high school algebra, a prerequisite for attempting the Army's prospective airman examination. By the time Frankie realized his error, he and his family had moved to San Jose. It made no difference to Uncle George where his pal lived. Every day for a month, George Lee journeyed over the narrow mountain road to tutor his friend. Not only did Frankie pass the exam, he became a career officer, retiring as a full colonel 30 years later.

Uncle George also is the first Chinese person to work a "visible" job at a white-owned, Santa Cruz business. He has a wonderful position at Webber's Photo Shop, and the adults around the Sunday table listen in silence to his stories about the interesting people who come into the store. "President Hoover's

George Lee, working with Rolleiflex 2.8C
at Webber's Photo Shop, Santa Cruz: 1948.

brought money to town. The story was right: Business is good. "The cannery workers have so much money, they buy beer, potato chips and candy for the kids without an afterthought," he says. "Can you believe I had $100 in sales one day last week?"

Dad is five-foot-five and 135 pounds of muscle. In the Army, he always won his battalion agility/strength tests and almost every day he carries 250 pound sides of beef from the delivery truck to the store's icebox. His customers are friendly "working people" and he is always having arm wrestling contests with them. He rarely loses to his bigger, heavier clientele.

Mom works right alongside Dad. She is always cheerful and energetic. Only five-foot-two, she covers a lot of ground in the shortest amount of time. As a youngster, she routinely walked six miles from Chinatown to Wilder Ranch to deliver Chinese medicines and foodstuffs to her father and had to walk fast to get there and back before dark.

Mother comes to Sunday dinner with bounty for me and my two-year-old brother, David: a basket of delicious overripe peaches and pears, apples with a few brown spots here and there, and the ends of bolognas and salamis that couldn't be sold but tasted as succulent as their expensive center cuts.

Mom misses me and my brother, and looks at us with sad eyes when she and Dad drive off after dinner.

Uncle Hong is thinking of starting a fruit stand in Soquel, he says. He makes this announcement in equal parts English and Toisanese—the usual mixture of languages around the dinner table. Toisanese is the rough country dialect of rural Guangdong Province, which lies halfway between the urban centers of Hong Kong and Canton, where they speak a smooth Cantonese dialect they deem vastly sweeter and superior to our country bumpkin sounds.

Uncle Hong is built like a small-sized football player but always plays down troubles in his quiet, understated way. He claims that he and his father are "outgrowing" a family grocery business they share with cousins. "My dad and Lam Sing are having some

niece came in today," he says in his matter-of-fact voice. "She bought a new Rolleiflex."

"She's nice," Uncle George would add, pausing before the punch line. "And pretty, too."

Ed Webber was a smart man, a fair man, a brave man. He was a Marine who went to naval photography school with Uncle George; he knew Uncle George was an expert with cameras and would make a top-notch employee. Ed Webber took a chance on hiring a Chinese person to clerk at the front counter of his store, and Uncle George came through, serving as both a pathfinder and an inspiration for the changing Chinatown community.

Around the table, Mom and Dad talk about their small Monterey store. We stay with Grandma and the aunts and uncles in Chinatown and only see Mom and Dad on Sundays. Dad read that the Monterey economy was strong because huge sardine catches disagreements," he says. "I think it's time to start our own business." What Uncle Hong is really saying is that the two men have argued violently over business.

Uncle Hong is married to Mom's sister, Auntie Ro, and is Dad's first cousin. He really is a Lam, but he is a Wong in America. Dad really is a Lam, too, but an Ow in America. The way this came about is a fairly common story among Chinese who wanted to immigrate to America but found themselves faced with the Chinese exclusion acts of the late nineteenth century. Both men came over on false papers bought in China and entered the U.S. claiming to be relatives of those for whom the papers were intended—Chinese who were acceptable for immigration through previous residence in the U.S. or family ties. All of this name-switching is a family secret because it can mean possible deportation if the authorities find out about it.

Others around the table include Uncle Wee, who just graduated from Santa Cruz High and bought a car that he is always working on, and Uncle Young and Auntie Lu, Santa Cruz High School students. They are "live wires" and speak mostly English. Auntie Lu is pretty, vivacious and athletic. "Tiny is running for GAA president, and I'm going to run as secretary," she says, always dreaming, always planning. If she were white, she would be homecoming queen.

Seated next to Lu, Uncle Young talks about basketball and his paper route. "I delivered all my papers in one hour and 25 minutes yesterday—a new world record. I was riding my bike 100 miles an hour and flipping papers on lawns at the same time."

Through all this teenage talk, Uncle Wee sits silently—until, that is, someone asks him about his new used car. He is well mannered and quiet, with a *pachuco* haircut and loose Levis that seem ready to fall off his hips. Poa and the old folks think he is a disgrace to the family, but he just smiles shyly and ignores their comments.

Next to Uncle Wee sits Uncle Jun, who attends Mission Hill Junior High School and delivers the *Santa Cruz Sentinel* every afternoon. He owns a won-

derful Red Ryder BB gun. We are friends and go off together while the adults talk. "I shot two robins and a small brown bird with some yellow feathers on the chest today," he says. "Let's go down to the river and spear some salmon."

Today, Dad's mother and her sister, Auntie Anna, have come to the dinner with my cousins Don and Allan, all of them dressed in their Sunday best. My cousins are a few years older than me, but we have a lot of fun playing cowboys and Indians and hide-and-go-seek in the bushes by the river. Their father is stuck in China because he can't get the papers to come to America.

Grandpa Lee presides over Sunday dinner with Poa. He is old, tall, stooped and as thin as a curved bamboo branch. He walks very slowly and seems ancient and creaky. He smokes Bull Durham cigarettes and always has a small five-cent bag of tobacco and some rolling papers nearby.

Grandpa Lee worked as a cook in America for over 50 years. His last job was a 20-year stint at Wilder Ranch, just north of town. When Wilder was made into a state park several years ago, I went on one of the tours. The main house had nice family rooms and a large kitchen, which served both family and workers. Next to the kitchen was a room called "the Chinese cook's room." This was where my grandfather lived six of seven days every week for 20 years, while Poa raised the seven kids in Chinatown.

Grandpa Lee always seems to be in a grouchy mood and doesn't like me playing with his things. But I do anyway. From going through his possessions on the table beside his narrow army-surplus cot, I know that he has only one silver Mercury-head dime and two brown Lincoln pennies to his name.

The Old Men

There were once a lot of the old men like Grandpa Lee in Santa Cruz's Chinatown. By 1947, however,

Ed Webber photo of Moon Lai Bok and George Ow, Jr.: 1947.

United States. But laws and secret covenants devised by the white majority made sure the Chinese could not gain social or economic equality with the city fathers. If these lonely old men had been white, some might have become a Leland Stanford, a Charles Crocker, a Cyrus Huntington or a Mark Hopkins. But they were Chinese and specifically legislated against in hundreds of ways. They and their fellow Chinese did heroic work for America. Their sweat built the railroads that linked America's two coasts. Their muscle was used in the mines, kitchens, factories and cramped back workrooms needed to build California and the West.

When the work was done, these men were no longer wanted and were prodded—many times brutally—to leave. So they went from the sardine docks of Monterey to the lettuce fields of Salinas, from the cantaloupe harvests of Yuma to the apple orchards of Washington, from the asparagus crops of Stockton to the strawberry patches of Watsonville, from the fish canneries of Alaska to the avocado groves of San Diego.

Now these old men are at the end of their line. Not having families or children of their own, the old men are gentle and playful with the few Chinese children in Chinatown. Grandpa Lee is at the end of his life, too, but he has established a family here. He has beaten laws aimed specifically at stopping Chinese women from coming to America and starting Chinese families.

While many European Americans look back at Ellis Island on the East Coast with fond memories, the Chinese look at Angel Island, their place of embarkation, as a prison where white people humiliated them and tried to send them—especially the women—back to China. There was little hope of a Chinese male in America starting a Chinese family. And if Chinese women weren't available, antimiscegenation laws made it illegal for Chinese men to "mix" with white women. The men knew that if they broke those laws, they could easily be lynched.

So, the old men are bachelors and my unofficial uncles. They have not seen Chinese children for so

the few left are dying off, one by one. Chin Lai, Ah Fook, Yee Hen and Lee Lam are quiet, competent old men. They know where to get free fish heads, how to cook dandelion and mustard greens they pick in empty lots, where to get mussels and clams at low tide, how to make tofu. They darn their own clothes and keep themselves company. They enjoy precious strands of tobacco gleaned from cigarette butts found on the sidewalk. They gather the tobacco in Prince Albert cans and roll their own.

Mostly, these old men spend their days sitting in the cool, shadowy quiet of the old tong hall, which is decorated with pictures of Sun Yat Sen, Abraham Lincoln, George Washington and Chiang Kai Shek. The Nationalist Chinese flag and the stars and stripes are tacked side by side on one wall. Once, this hall was filled with hopeful, energetic young Chinese men wanting to make their fame and fortune on "Gold Mountain," which is what the Chinese called the long that I am a wonder to them. They give me sweets and firecrackers. They see in my youthful hope and my father's adult strength the dreams, the aspirations of their young manhoods. I can see the strength that once coursed through their bodies, but now they are slow and old—like the spent salmon that littered the San Lorenzo River after spawning—shells of what they once were, ready to pass on.

When my father was in the Army and other Chinese people had jobs in the Kaiser shipbuilding plant in Oakland, Chin Lai looked at Dad and said, "You were born at the right time." Chin Lai meant that while his generation could only get migrant agricultural, cannery and hard-labor jobs, World War II had made it possible for the Chinese to secure good-paying employment. But for Chin Lai—and the other old men—his statement acknowledged that it was too late for them.

I am even luckier than my dad. In 1943, the year I was born, the anti-Chinese Laws are beginning to crumble. After all, China is America's ally in the war against fascism and it is bad public relations to have overtly racist laws against the friend fighting beside you. Dad will eventually become a citizen, vote, own land, have rights in court—in other words, "become legal." My siblings and I will be able to go to college and work shoulder to shoulder with whites in any occupation we choose, a situation that was unimaginable to my grandparents and only a hopeful dream to my mother and father. I definitely was born under a lucky star.

Other Voices, Other Faces

Hock Guey, or "black people," live in Chinatown, too. Black men reside in a boardinghouse across the street from Poa's and work at various jobs around town. There is my friend Oscar, one year younger than I, who moved next door to us from the South.

He is slim, relaxed, slow-moving and honey-skinned. We roam around Chinatown together. We know where all the cherry plum trees are in Chinatown. Sometimes we fill small brown bags full of sweet and juicy plums and sell them at the Greyhound Bus Station, two blocks east of Chinatown, for a nickel or a dime a bag.

There is always the San Lorenzo River to play in, with steelhead swimming upstream during the winter rains. In summer, all the water in the river disappears, except for a trickle in the middle of the channel. In a dry year, there would be but occasional pools of water filled with slimy and snake-scary eels. Oscar and I laugh and chase each other along the sandy river bottom, exploring the world of birds and fish and insects from one season to another, with no sense of ourselves as marginalized or living in a ghetto.

The World Outside

The city beyond Chinatown and my play world on the banks of the San Lorenzo River was both strange and dangerous. You could get lost. There were tall buildings made of hard stone, not of softly weathered wood like the houses in Chinatown. There were cement sidewalks and hard streets. In Chinatown, there were a few wooden sidewalks but China Lane was a rock-studded dirt pathway.

The white faces outside Chinatown seemed expressionless and clenched. There were no friendly smiles on yellow, brown and black faces. Outside of Chinatown, there were mean white boys who called you names and beat you up for no reason other than that you were Chinese.

When I started kindergarten at Laurel Elementary School (now the Louden Nelson Community Center), I still spoke a gibberish of Toisanese-Cantonese and English. This was even more problematic than it might have been in another place because everyone in the school was white except me and Uncle Jun, who was in the sixth grade. My teacher told my parents to speak English to me if they wanted me to do well in school.

In the cafeteria, teachers made me eat all my food, even though it sometimes tasted strange. Recesses were horrible. Packs of kids would tease and chase me, yelling, "Chin, Chin, Chinaman." There were too many of them to fight.

I stopped going out for recess. My teacher was kind and knew what was happening. I stayed in the classroom and read. She gave me a book called *Sandy the Dog,* which I loved and read again and again. Eventually, I read every book on the class bookshelf. I then got permission to get books from the school library down the hall. I believe I was the only one in my class who had this privilege—and, probably, the only one who wanted it.

I especially loved the biographies of great Americans: George Washington, Abraham Lincoln, Betsy Ross, Dolly Madison, Daniel Boone. They all were brave and faced hard times, just as I was facing them. They always did the right thing and were heroes. I wanted to be like them.

If I had a good book, it didn't matter how many mean kids there were on the playground or that I didn't go to recess. I could be a soldier with George Washington at Valley Forge and part of the winning side at Yorktown. I could be sitting with Betsy Ross in front of her Philadelphia fireplace as she sewed the first American flag. I could be helping Dolly Madison move things out of the White House before the British burned it during the War of 1812. I could be anywhere and I could do great things.

When I grew older, my room would be full of books, and libraries and book stores would be my favorite places. Love of reading would eventually get me through Monterey High School, Monterey Peninsula Junior College, San Francisco State College and UCLA, from which I received my MBA. Reading, information and knowledge have made life a joy and helped me to succeed in my business career.

Chinatown Sunset

The beginning of the end of Chinatown started with people moving out and concluded with a flood and the redevelopment of the area into a shopping center. By the time of the 1955 flood, only my grandmother and her new husband, Maneleno Serna, called Chinatown home. Poa gave her new husband the name "Arnold" and that is what everyone in the family affectionately called him. He was a warmhearted man from the Philippines who smoked a pipe and enjoyed a beer—when my grandmother would let him have one. He had served in the United States Army during World War II and had worked many years in the fields.

Uncle Jun was going to Lassen Junior College in far-off Susanville in 1955. He was studying gunsmithing. By then, the old men had died and younger Chinese could earn good wages and routinely buy homes outside of Chinatown. Many homes and subdivisions still had restrictive covenants saying that people of the "Mongolian race"—as well as Negroes and Jews—could not buy or live in those communities. Although the discriminating codes were only selectively enforced, it would not be until the civil rights struggles of the 1960s that the racial and religious barriers finally would be torn down.

By 1955, I lived with Mom and Dad in Monterey, a few blocks above Cannery Row, and helped operate our "little gold mine" grocery store. Uncle George, Auntie Priscilla and their daughter, Patti, lived in a new house on South Branciforte Avenue. Auntie Ro and Uncle Hong and their children, Linda and Ronnie, lived on Glenview Avenue. Uncle Young had drowned in a rain-swollen Trinity River while fishing in 1948, and Auntie Lu was in Germany with her

Chinatown Sunset: 1941.

new husband, Uncle Bob Yien, who was a captain in the Army Dental Corps.

George Liu had bought the New Monterey Market in Monterey after working for my father for a while. Uncle Wee was in Monterey, too, living a half-block below us, while Auntie Anna, Grandma Lam and Donny, Allan and Nancy still lived on Younglove Street in Westside Santa Cruz.

Our Chinatown was almost empty, and many of the old buildings had been torn down.

I was in the seventh grade during that winter of '55. December had been rainy and, several days before Christmas, there was talk that the San Lorenzo River might flood. We decided to drive up to Santa Cruz from Monterey to see how Poa and Arnold were doing. It was raining and Uncle Wee, who had a day off from his cook's job at Fort Ord, drove us—my father was too busy taking care of the store to come along.

When we turned from Front Street into Chinatown, I saw a raging river at the end of China Lane. The river had overflowed its banks and was chewing up big chunks of grandma's garden. Slabs of earth as large as cars caved in and were carried away by the speeding water. Giant redwood trees, parts of houses and even small buildings swept past. A car floated by, and then another one. The river had become a gigantic onslaught of water, and seemed to be growing larger and more powerful as I watched. Only a miracle could save Chinatown.

Poa was uncharacteristically subdued. She had been through this before, a few times in Santa Cruz, a few in China. Chinatown's fate was in the hands of the gods, her calmness seemed to say.

The rain kept falling. Around midnight on Christmas, there was a high tide. The ocean surge pushed up the mouth of the San Lorenzo River near the roller coaster, creating a tidal bore that kept the river from flowing freely into Monterey Bay. Uncle George Lee made sure everyone was out of Poa's house, then opened the front and back doors to allow the flooding

The end of Chinatown—the December 1955 Flood. Jun Lee (left, in hip waders) and George Lee (right) in the floodwaters at Pacific Avenue and Church Street, Santa Cruz. Photo by Ed Webber.

waters to enter and exit the building, thereby making sure that the house didn't float away. Then he and Uncle Jun went to Webber's Photo Shop to move inventory from the basement and first floor to the second story. By the time they left the store, the river was as high as the parking meters and five men had to link arms to get across the street.

After the flood, Uncle George sold the Lee family land to the Santa Cruz Redevelopment Agency and built Poa, Arnold and Uncle Jun a house on Pine Street, a few blocks from both his home and Auntie Ro's house. The big dinners would continue at Poa's new home and in the big house that Auntie Lu and Uncle Bob would build on Fairland Way near De Laveaga.

Keith Shaffer, Cliff Swenson and others would construct a shopping center where Chinatown once stood, complete with a Longs Drugs and an Albertson's supermarket. We were one generation away from doing that ourselves. Even though we didn't know it then, we were learning…and preparing.

World War II and Korea

George Lee while at naval photography school, Pensacola, Florida: 1943.

Tonkinese selling grass skirts, Espiritu Santo, New Hebrides Islands: 1944.

Laundry day in Sumar,
Philippine Islands: 1945.

Islanders on canoe, Espiritu
Santo, New Hebrides Islands:
1944.

George Lee's quarters at Espiritu Santo,
New Hebrides Islands: 1944.

Kim Wong, Army photo: 1944.

Two men, New Hebrides Islands: 1944.

Man with pipe and pig,
New Hebrides Islands: 1944.

Four islanders on a canoe, New Hebrides Islands: 1944.

Robert Chase, George Lee and Robert Nelson, Espiritu Santo, New Hebrides Islands: 1944.

CHINATOWN DREAMS

YWCA, Honolulu, Hawai'i:
1944.

R&R, Honolulu, Hawai'i, with
Seventh Division troopers just
back from Kwajalein: 1944.

George Lee with F-56 Aerial Camera, Shelton, Washington: 1945.

CHINATOWN DREAMS

TOP
George Lee with a child,
Honolulu, Hawai'i: 1944.

BOTTOM
Victory Dinner, Seattle Chinatown,
just after VJ Day: 1945.

Chinese USO, Seattle, Washington: 1944.

George Ow holding baby David with
Emily Lee Ow and George Ow, Jr.,
Santa Cruz Chinatown: 1945.

George Ow returned from WWII: 1945.

George Lee, Aviation Photographer's Mate, Second Class, with Leica; Philadelphia Naval Yard: 1950.

AF2 George Lee, Miss Indiana and AF2 John Lucas of Yonkers, New York;
Miss America Contest, Atlantic City, New Jersey: 1951.

JAMES D. HOUSTON

East Side, West Side, All Around the Town

Back in the late 1920s, when George Lee was a youngster, he met some descendants of James Frazier Reed, co-organizer of the legendary Donner Party. Before long he had become a friend of the family, and they offered him important encouragement when he first showed an interest in photography. It is a Santa Cruz story. It is a cross-cultural story. It is the story of California pioneers coming from opposite directions—one family from Canton, in southern China, one from Ireland, by way of Illinois—to meet here on East Cliff Drive at the edge of the Pacific. And it starts with a missing candy bar.

James Frazier Reed was born in 1800 and had crossed the Atlantic to the United States as a young boy, with his widowed mother. Forty-six years later when he started west with his wife and four children,

at the head of a wagon train, he was an immigrant again, bound for what was then a northern province of Mexico.

Two generations went by, and Reed's grandson, James Frazier Lewis, grew up in Capitola-by-the Sea, just south of Santa Cruz, becoming wealthy in the candy business. He developed the world's first nickel candy bar, called the Frazier Lewis Victoria Cream. By 1915 he had made enough money to buy a steep-roofed estate house in the Twin Lakes district, still sometimes known as "The Frazier Lewis House." His mother, Patty Reed Lewis, the younger daughter of James F. Reed and one of the Donner Party's better-known survivors, spent her final years in this house, where she passed away in 1923. By the late '20s it was occupied by Frazier Lewis, two of his sisters, and a Chinese cook named Wong, who lived on the ground floor.

From time to time Mr. Wong would visit China-town, near the river, to shop, to gamble, to call on friends. He always brought along pockets full of candy, which he passed around to the youngsters in the neighborhood. On one of these visits, sometime in 1928 or 1929, Mr. Wong's supply ran out just before he reached seven-year-old George Lee, who was so disappointed that Mr. Wong promised him he'd have his piece of candy before the day was done. When it came time to catch the bus back to the Eastside, he brought the lad along.

For young George, it was a historic trip. He had seldom traveled east of the San Lorenzo River, nor had there been much reason to. The family's life was centered in the downtown Chinese community. George attended Laurel School, just a few blocks south. His father worked up the coast, as the cook at Wilder Ranch. Moreover, it was a long way, in those days, to the Twin Lakes district, which was still very rural, separated from the main part of Santa Cruz by a lot of open space.

Lee Family: Gue Shee Lee looking out from doorway. Foreground, left to right, Rose, Emily, Young, George and Wee.
The original Santa Cruz Dominican Hospital, now the Branciforte Plaza, is in the background: 1931. Photo by Alice Halsey.

"You could buy a live chicken just about anywhere," George recalls. "The Lewises themselves, they raised pigs. They had a pigpen right down there by the lake."

There was no shopping district yet, no small-craft harbor, nor any state park to look after the wildlife around Schwan Lagoon. The lagoon, in fact, was part of the sizable piece of property that surrounded the tall Victorian standing out there by itself about a block back from the beach, with gardens on one side and a pair of sheds on the other—a backyard candy factory, as George was soon to learn.

In his eyes this was a strange and exotic part of the world, and he did not intend to linger. At age seven his main objective was to get his Victoria Cream and head back home. "Any piece of candy was a big deal," he says, "especially one that cost a nickel. I remember in grade school when they asked for a nickel as a donation to the Red Cross, you had to think twice. In those days that was a lot of money."

Mr. Wong showed him around the place, let him peek inside the candy factory, where women sat at tables dipping confections into vats of chocolate. While George was on the premises, Mr. Wong decided to introduce him to the family. And much to George's surprise, they invited him to stay for lunch, about to be served in the dining room upstairs.

It was a high-ceilinged room, with redwood walls and moldings, with a tiled fireplace, stained-glass

73

window panels, and plate rails lined with China plates in the Blue Willow pattern. "I found out later," he says, "those plates really came from China."

Two mail-order catalogues were stacked on a chair so George could sit up high enough to eat at the table. At home he never used anything but chopsticks. He remembers that they showed him how to use a knife and fork. He remembers that French fries were served. And he remembers that there were cashew nuts, as many as he cared to eat. "They came from India," he says, "in a big five-gallon can. Somehow that really impressed me. Nuts all the way from India!"

In the years to come George would dine at this table many times. The Lewis family liked him instantly and took him in, as if he were the grandson they had often longed for. Of Patty Reed's eight children, three were then still living—Martha Jane Lewis was 65, James Frazier was 63, Susan Augusta was 59. They all lived together, and none of them had married.

After a few more visits they had given the young fellow the run of the place. And it was a delicious place for a boy to run around in, a mystery house full of side rooms, stairwells, nooks and crannies, with an attic upstairs, and a lookout tower. On one visit George happened to open a door and came upon a room where materials for the candy business were stored—shipping boxes, packages of wrappers, and some rather large chunks of chocolate brittle.

"This was like a hidden treasure," he says. "If you want to know the truth, I was never crazy about the taste of the Victoria Creams. They were pretty sweet, too rich. What I really liked was this chocolate mixed with brittle. A ten-pound chunk of that was quite a find."

In one of the ground-floor rooms there was another kind of hidden treasure. It had been a darkroom, where the sisters had stored some long-abandoned camera equipment. When they learned that George had taken an interest in photography, they told him to make use of it in any way he could.

"By that time," he says, "I must have been starting Santa Cruz High. One of my friends from the Boy Scouts, he was an Italian kid, had come over one day with two boxes and said, 'I'm going to show you how to print pictures.' 'Print pictures?' I said. 'What's that?' But from that day onward I was hooked. And thanks to the Lewises I rigged up my first enlarger. Earlier in life, one of the sisters had been an amateur photographer. In that room downstairs they had all this stuff that went clear back to the 1890s—albums, emulsion plates, old view cameras that you set up on tripods. One thing I did was take those plates and boil off the emulsion. You couldn't use them for picture taking any more. But they made great windows. The glass was from Czechoslovakia. Glass nowadays has a greenish tint. This was the clearest glass I'd ever seen. No tint. Pure light came through. Each panel was about eight by ten inches. I cleaned off all the emulsion and built some new windows into our house downtown. And around that same time I took one of the old view cameras apart and made an enlarger from the lenses and the bellows. I attached them to the ceiling in my bedroom at home. I used a coffee can to hold the light. Some of my earliest prints were enlarged with lenses that came out of the Lewis family storeroom in the 1930s."

A few years later, George was called upon to photograph a precious family heirloom. During high school he had stayed in touch with the Lewises. By this time—the early months of World War II—he was nearing twenty and would soon be enlisting in the Navy. Susan, the younger sister, had passed away. Frazier Lewis was failing. Martha Jane, now close to eighty, was making arrangements to donate various possessions to the museum at Sutter's Fort in Sacramento, including the single most famous artifact associated with the Donner Party saga.

The family Victorian had become a museum of its own, filled with generations of furniture, memorabilia and heirlooms, much of it linking the Lewises to the epic period of western settlement. There were diaries

James Reed had kept during the transcontinental crossing, documents he and John Sutter signed at the Fort, and land petitions from the 1840s, drafted by Reed after he decided to settle in Santa Clara Valley. There was a wedding dress Patty Reed wore when she and San Jose businessman Frank Lewis were married in 1856, and there was a four-inch ceramic doll that eight-year-old Patty had sewn into the lining of her skirt, unable to part with this memento of the world they'd left behind in Springfield, Illinois. After five months on the western trail the Reeds had lost all their oxen. In the Nevada desert they had to abandon their final wagon, along with all belongings. Secretly young Patty carried the doll with her through the harrowing winter of 1846/47, when 41 of the 87 members in the party starved to death, trapped in the snows below Donner Summit. The following spring, after the survivors made it down to the Sacramento Valley, she revealed the doll to rescuers, and it immediately became part of a story that would be told and retold for decades to come.

By the early 1940s Patty's doll had been often written about but seldom seen, stored away in the drawers and trunks that moved with James Reed's descendants from San Jose to Capitola to the Twin Lakes house on East Cliff Drive. The picture George had been asked to shoot was among the first ever taken of this now much photographed icon of the pioneer era.

So there they were—you can imagine the scene—George Lee, whose father had sailed from China to San Francisco Bay in the 1890s, and Martha Jane Lewis, whose Irish-born grandfather had been twice an immigrant. See them together in the living room paneled with heart redwood from nearby forests. It is 1941 or 1942. The big bay windows, facing south, are filled with light off Monterey Bay. They consider the shading, the angle of light. George crouches, lining up the shot. Martha adjusts the tiny skirt of the four-inch doll that has become the poignant symbol of a child's inextinguishable hope.

"I had a Zeiss by that time," George says. "It was a good German camera. I bought it at Montgomery Ward for $14.95, right toward the end of the Depression. That was quite an investment. You figure my father was making sixty dollars a month back then. I brought it over to the house, and Martha got out the doll. At the time I had no idea what I was photographing—I mean, the significance of it. I didn't know much at all about her family's history. I just did it as a favor for a woman with a kind heart who had been so hospitable all those years, and she needed a picture of something that had belonged to her mother. I didn't even keep the negative. I gave it to the people in San Francisco who were printing it up, for a catalogue or a booklet. But I remember the shot. I remember I got in as close as I could with that camera, so the whole doll filled the frame. It was black and white, taken in the front room. I haven't seen it since, though I think I would recognize it. Every time I see a picture of that doll I check the credit and wonder if it might be the one I took."

George didn't visit the house again. A short time later he was heading back across the ocean, the way his father had come, to serve as a U.S. Navy photographer in the South Pacific campaign. As was true in so many ways, those war years marked the end of one era, and the beginning of the next. While he was overseas the last Lewis passed away. When George finally got back to his hometown, the old house had changed hands, and Patty's doll had been transferred to Sutter's Fort, where it has now been on display for over 50 years.

TONY HILL

Sharing an American Dream

There is a single photograph in the collected work of George Lee that separates his work from virtually every other American photographer: it is the photograph of two young boys, one Chinese American, the other African American—an anomaly so significant, so immense, that I can think of no other similar image in the American experience. And I can think of no such image from my own childhood, growing up in Harlem, a world separate and apart from New York's Chinatown, long down the East River. In Harlem, the idea of having a Chinese American friend was unimaginable. The Chinese were foreign, mysterious—from a place I knew not where.

But in George Lee's world—in George Lee's Chinatown—the image appears so natural, the two young smiling children so organically linked, that one

David Lee Ow with Oscar Presley: Circa 1948.

the worlds in which these two young boys co-exist are also caught in a vortex of change. The Chinese Exclusion Act of 1882, which targeted Chinese immigrants during a period of Sinophobic hysteria, had just been repealed in 1943. California's antimiscegenation law—which would have prevented both David and Oscar from marrying women of European descent—would be found unconstitutional by the California Supreme Court in 1948.

The late 1940s also marked the emergence of Jackie Robinson as a national hero, particularly for black Americans like myself. His courage and tenacity in the "national pastime" acted as a wake-up call to end white-only privilege, culminating in the Supreme Court's landmark decision, *Brown v. Board of Education,* in 1954. The photograph at once frames that moment and illuminates it: joy inside of darkness, dreams against all odds.

I also see a little bit of myself in young Oscar—happy-go-lucky on the outside, but inside uncertain of what the future holds. I would become one of the first black Americans bused to an all-white school in the aftermath of the court's decision, and I recall with great clarity the anxiety and uncertainty of my first bus rides. In a very real sense, the photo prefigures the multicultural America imagined by that decision.

The reality, of course, is something else again. Chinese Americans, while accessing economic and educational advantages, remain the targets of white stereotypes and prejudices. Black Americans, particularly young black males, remain caught in a world that remains separate and unequal. A pernicious institutional racism pervades American society, so much so that a young black male born today is more likely to go to prison than to college.

More than a half-century after it was taken, George Lee's photograph reminds us of the American conundrum about race. It provides a benchmark for both what we can be and what we have yet to become. The dream is still unrealized—and yet it must still be dreamed.

needs to look twice at the photo to grasp its significance. David Ow, George Lee's nephew, with roots stretching across the Pacific to Canton, and Oscar Presley, with his roots stretching across the American continent and the Atlantic all the way to the Euphrates, sharing in the joys of childhood, sharing in laughter, sharing in their dreams, American dreams, all in a multicultural American "Chinatown."

The photograph, like Lee's other Chinatown works, is immediate and filled with humanity and compassion. It provides a rare glimpse at the human spirit. It also provides a rare glimpse into a peculiar moment in American history.

In a very real sense, the boys are united by the ways in which Asian and African Americans were targeted at the time by mainstream white racism and everyday prejudices. They are "allies" in their marginalization. Taken, however, in the immediate aftermath of World War II—my guess is somewhere around 1947 or 1948—

Community Portraits

Miss California Pageant, Santa Cruz Beach
Boardwalk: Circa 1950.

Ernest Otto at George Lee's wedding dinner: 1949.

Rock Cod Lines, Santa Cruz Wharf: 1941.

CHINATOWN DREAMS

Twin Lakes Beach, Santa Cruz: 1950.

82

Supreme Court Building, Washington, D.C.: 1951.

CHINATOWN DREAMS

Hoy Lew at age 92. Portrait session, Cabrillo College: Circa 1990.

She Stands

Tears flow down Anna's cheeks the day the sold sign is removed. The front door key burns in her palm. The year is 1947, and the house is one of an expanse of white cookie-cutter homes along Younglove Avenue in Santa Cruz, California. The development stands out among the pastel one-story bungalows of neighboring streets. Sure, it's a simple structure—a box divided into four equal rooms with a tiny bathroom at its center, surely an afterthought. "But it's all mine," she reminds herself.

Anna pictures its grass carpet, rolled out like a welcome mat from the foundation, tickling the feet of her sons, Allan and Donny, as they play cowboys and Indians. At eight and six years old, respectively, they have never had the luxury of a lawn to stain their hand-me-down overalls, a simple pleasure every kid deserves.

Lam Pon Family, just before returning to China—George (who would return to the United States in 1937 as George Ow), Mrs. Lam Pon (Lam Ow High), Lam Pon, Anna Lam (who had just graduated from Santa Cruz High School, Class of 1930): 1930.

With just a few extra hours stocking cans, chopping meats and maintaining the books at the corner mart, Anna figures she can afford the $2,500 asking price and pay back the mortgage loan within a few months. It's easy work compared with crouching all day picking strawberries, which she did last season, or peeling apples, which she did the season before. She prefers to stand.

Her mom—affectionately called *Poi* by the children—will oversee the youngsters and ensure a hot meat-and-vegetable meal is served when the family gathers around the table at seven o'clock that night. Anna sees how happy the boys make Poi, and how she

spoils them in return with treats of deep-fried sweets and games of catch. Besides, Poi cries less when preoccupied with thoughts other than of her own private suffering back in China: the pain of loving a husband who had taken a younger wife into her mother's old home, started another family and disrespectfully shifted Poi's framed photograph on the wall beneath that of the second wife. Anna understands how the life she provides for her mother is at least respectful and loving.

"Come on, Annie, face this way!" says brother-in-law Georgie, who has called her Annie since she was a kid. So "Annie" it will always be, even though she now pushes 35. He points to the camera lens, raises it to eye level, then sings, "Say money!"

Georgie adds, "Let's put on a nice smile for George."

George. Her heart stops at the sound of his name, because it both pleases and shocks her, hearing it aloud when family and friends have avoided mentioning his name—especially when the boys are around—as a sign of respect for her loss. Her memory pumps the blood through her body until at last she catches her breath and her heart resumes its steady pace. She pats her dark pin curls into place, then smiles into her compact mirror, making sure her red lipstick hasn't faded.

Anna still considers herself a newlywed, even though she hasn't seen George in six years—or is it seven? It's funny how the years meld into one amorphous span of time when you are too busy surviving and forgetting sorrows as months click by.

She turns and gathers Allan and Donny, gently cupping their shoulders from behind, not noticing their mugging expressions or how the hands in their pockets accentuate their squirming. The snap of the camera shutter preserves the moment: her private triumph in owning a piece of the American Dream.

"You've managed to raise such great kids, Annie," Georgie says, dropping the camera so it hangs suspended from the strap around his neck.

"Don't forget smart, too," she chuckles, "even fluent in Chinese, thanks to my mom, which is better than I can say for myself."

"They take after you. Say, how is George doing?" This time the sound of George's name rattles her, obscuring the question momentarily, since she is not accustomed to hearing it twice in the same conversation, let alone hearing it at all.

"He's doing all he can, considering . . . ," she says. "Say, let me show you my palace." Turning the key in the deadbolt, Anna is both surprised and pleased at the sound of the metallic click as the barrel flips over.

She inhales the wet-paint smell as though it were the finest perfume and is taken aback by the bright-

Anna Lam Liu with sons, Allan and Donny, at house on Younglove Avenue, Santa Cruz: 1948.

ness of the walls, which makes the rooms appear larger and taller. The beam of sunlight drawn through the yellow curtains of the picture window casts a warm hue on everything it touches, including the squealing boys, each busy staking out his desired room. Georgie follows the threesome inside, asking decorating questions, snapping shots of the trio's grand-gestured responses, capturing the wonder of the new surroundings and the moment.

Staring at the kitchen, Anna remembers how she met George at a friend's dinner party when she was 22, during her last year at Canton's Lingnan University.

She studied Chinese history, a major girls were allowed to study, with literature, math and science afforded only to boys. Her father, the successful owner of a Santa Cruz apple-drying company, had brought the family back to China so that Anna could learn the language and forget the ways American culture had tainted her early years.

If Anna picked out a husband along the way, that was an added bonus. Besides, she was ready to marry. She recalls the "village-thinking" her mother had pounded into her over many years. If you were a woman who failed to marry, you were nothing. And when you died, your unrealized and unwanted body would be given suitable burial near the outhouse. She couldn't picture anything so gruesome.

George was 30, a radio repair technician with a chiseled face accentuated by slicked-back ebony hair. He spoke English well compared to others she had met, and surprised her when he got excited with his shouts of "Blimey!"—a remnant of a childhood spent in Australia. Exotic and interesting, he told stories of white sandy beaches—a land where people were welcoming and friendly, and the sweet fruit hung from trees, looking so delicious and begging to be picked.

He liked her smile. A Mona Lisa half-smile that intrigued him both in what it showed and what it held back. What wasn't she saying? She, too, was worldly, having grown up in the United States. He loved listening to her stories about being the first Chinese woman to graduate from Santa Cruz High, admiring her strength. They courted for two years, then married, to the joy of both families who lived in neighboring villages in Toisan.

It all seemed so simple then.

She marvels now at her two sons who seem so well adjusted, so American. What a prize to be doubly blessed with good fortune! Allan and Donny are sweaty, their bangs pressed to their foreheads, having run between rooms and into closets. They have discovered the bathroom, turning the chrome faucet on and off, fighting over who gets to flush the toilet next.

George Liu at Coit Tower, San Francisco: 1949.

Georgie chuckles after declaring that it's his turn, settling the argument and diverting their attention to something new.

George had never seen young Donny, who was always two paces behind his big brother. Mimicking Allan's every move, Donny was now flicking light switches on and off. His face, the way he tipped back his head in laughter, evokes Anna's memory of George. It is painful now for her to draw the connection. She smiles, knowing how pleased George would have been to see his miniature self.

Anna recalls the last time she touched George's face, long after the laughing had stopped. She and George had been relaxing after dinner in their living room, burping Allan while listening to a radio that George fixed with odd parts after it was deemed irreparable by a customer. An announcement crackled through the speaker, changing history and their lives together forever: "Japan has invaded Manchuria!"

"You have got to leave this place," George said. "The war is coming and it's not safe anymore. Take Allan and go!" He smoothed his hands on his pants, stood up and began pacing. Allan wailed on cue, as though he understood, settling down only when she patted his back. Anna glanced down at her breasts, which drooped like burlap sacks of rice onto her protruding belly, round with child and getting rounder. She grasped for alternatives, but they both knew there was only one. She had to leave.

"Anna, you'll have a much better chance in America. You're a U.S. citizen, remember, unlike me," George implored. "They will let you go as a woman bearing a child. Besides, if the three of you have a chance, I will be able to sleep at night. Don't you have uncles you can stay with?"

He stroked her cheek, catching the tears on his fingers. He forced a tight-lipped smile, hoping her mirrored expression would reassure them both that everything was going to be okay. She imagined her heart being sucked into her stomach, little feet trampling on whatever life was left.

Anna left Hong Kong on a passenger ship, the *President Coolidge,* bound for Angel Island, with Allan bundled in one arm and a suitcase in the other, not knowing what would come next.

Letters would arrive monthly from George, beginning with the words "Dearest Anna" and ending with "I'll be there soon." Written with a sense of hope, it was as though he were on a great sightseeing journey and reporting in at key way stations. It was easier like that. He was living with a bunch of buddies in the interior of China, repairing radio stations for the government. He had hoped personal connections with officials would make a difference.

Saving his money to buy a ticket to America, George carefully set aside extra for bribe money if needed. But Anna knew as well as he did that the Chinese Exclusion Act, which forbade all but a trickle of Chinese from entering the country each year, was like playing the lottery, one chance in a million. You didn't get more chances if you had hopes and dreams, a family that desperately missed you or a son who had never seen your face nor heard your voice.

Anna had hope, a beautiful home and a family.

Her mind fades back into the room where she has been standing for some time. The boys crowd around her, Allan grabbing her waist, and Donny her thigh, as though her body were a great tree filled with branches of old and new growth. She squeezes back and tousles their shiny black heads. They glance up smiling, the warmth of the room returning to their faces.

"C'mon," she says, "let's go see what Poi has made us for lunch and tell her which room is hers!" With that, the boys swing the front door open, run into the yard and collapse together into a giggling mound on the lawn. Anna turns and follows Georgie, now looking exhausted from the boys pulling at his jacket, to show him parts of the house he hasn't seen. She glances back into the house before twisting the key, knowing that it is perfect, knowing that the boys will be happy here, knowing which walls to knock down in order to add on another bedroom when George comes home.

For now, Anna will enclose in a letter the photo Georgie took this afternoon—one showing her husband how big the boys are, how pretty the Younglove house is, and everything he has waiting for him.

Chinatown Farewell

TOP
1940 Chinatown Flood. "The water came right up to
the doorsteps of our house," said George Lee.

BOTTOM LEFT
Drying out after the December 1955 Flood: 1956.

BOTTOM RIGHT
Chinatown houses being demolished: 1956.

92

Gambling houses being demolished: 1956.

Gambling houses being demolished: 1956.

CHINATOWN DREAMS

The Photographer Remembers

Fishing boats in a foggy bay;
a lone cypress on a hill
high above a blustery sea;
the river rising, its surface
slurred by sunlight and wind;
and always the slab-board houses
and their rickety stairs
that we thought would shiver
into piles of broken wood
at the start of every storm:
I remember all these things—
incidents, family, friends.
I can even see the wharf
and the old silent men
who sat on crates and fished,
looking toward another shore.
I see them in my head:
the tottering houses,
the dirt streets and boxy cars,
the women hanging wash
on shadowy porches in the rain,
women who every now and then,
like the old silent men,
would stop to stare at something

95

beyond the river and the bay,
beyond the border of here
and there, their faces cracking
like dinner plates as they fought
against the surge of tears.

Those faces were not only
from a different time
but from a different place,
the other side of daylight
where the wind would call to me
with the voices of relatives
long dead, mothers of mothers,
fathers of old silent men.
My days have been crowded
with these relatives of wind,
with family and friends
and ghosts who each night
shake the window frames
as if wanting to get in.

At odd moments, as in a dream,
stores demolished long ago
will emerge from the fog
like overturned boats,
or rain-whipped hillsides
above a river bank will shake
into the ghostly shapes of houses
from whose windy rooms
I hear the murmurings
of half-remembered voices.
I reach toward those voices,
toward those faces
from the other side of light,
but they fall through my grasp,
and I turn away, knowing
that only the fingers of an ocean
can touch the shorelines
of two continents
at the same time.

Old country, middle kingdom
at my back and in my head,
you are a presence that pushes
me forward, whose ways I won't
and can't forget. Everything
I am and will become
is what you were and what
my parents carried
to this foreign place
that is as much my home now
as that distant land
of long-dead ancestors
and old silent men.
Ghosts still shake the windows,
but there is as much
reality for me
in the sun-slurred river
gliding to the sea, and in
the women hanging wash
on clapboard porches,
as much meaning in gulls
hovering in mid-flight or herons
standing motionless on shore,
as in the murmuring wind
that mutters outside my door.

Not a day or week goes by,
however, that I don't see
in my photographs of baby
nieces and school-girl friends
the mothers and aunts
they will become, or don't detect
beneath wrinkles and double chins
the infant features
of uncles and boys
and so many I know now
as grandfathers
and middle-aged sons.
Not a day or week goes by
that squawking gulls who poke

and flap in the tidal mud
don't remind me
of family and friends,
and I don't observe
in the staring eyes
of stoop-shouldered heron—
standing skinny-legged
in a marsh or riverbed—
the stares of ancient women
and the gaze of old silent men.

Family Album

No. 1122751

Chinese passport with photo, Wong Family—Lucille, Joong Seu, Priscilla: 1939.

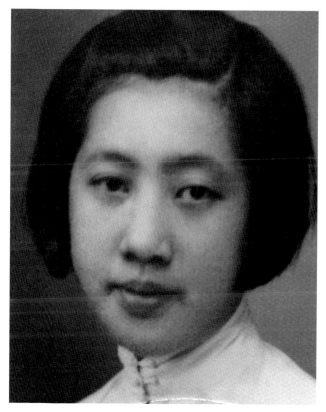

TOP LEFT
George Wong, immigration photo: 1924.

TOP RIGHT
Young Margery Woo with her uncle, Raymond
Woo: Circa 1927.

BOTTOM RIGHT
Margery Woo, high school graduation photo, China:
Late 1930s.

Joong Seu Wong with daughters Priscilla, Lucille and Georgina, Santa Cruz: 1948.

George Lee and Priscilla Wong: 1947:

Watching a Santa Cruz parade with George Liu (center) standing behind (left to right) his sons, Donny and Allan, with Georgina Wong and Priscilla Wong Lee in front of Webber's Photo Shop: 1949.

George Lee with Georgina Wong, at Santa Cruz City Hall: 1947.

CHINATOWN DREAMS

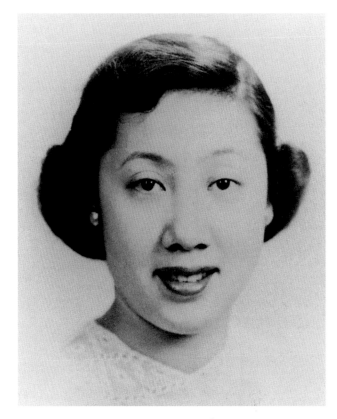

Margery Woo with relatives in state of Washington: Early 1950s.

Margery Woo passport photo: 1949.

George Ow with David Lee Ow:
1947.

George Ow, Sr., with George, Jr.,
and David: Circa 1947.

George Ow with David and
George, Jr., at Santa Cruz Beach:
1950.

Gary Ow, George Ow and Bing
Yue Ow in front of the Gary
Brothers Market in Gadsden,
Arizona: Early 1950s.

TOP
Chinatown Dinner: 1949.

BOTTOM
Ow and Lam-Liu Families,
Chinatown Santa Cruz: 1950.

Sisters Priscilla Wong Lee and Georgina Wong at Christmas: 1950.

Extended family picture taken at Santa Cruz City Hall, with ivy-covered Carnegie Library
in background: 1949.

Gue Shee Lee with grandchildren Terry Ow and Linda Wong: 1950.

Ow-Lam-Liu Families, Monterey, California: 1954.

CHINATOWN DREAMS

Family of George and Joong Seu Wong, Santa Cruz: 1959.

CHINATOWN DREAMS

Four generations—Mrs. Lam Pon (Lam Ow High) and her son, George Ow, grandson David Lee Ow, and great-granddaughter Karen Ow; Monterey, California: 1963.

Gue Shee Lee and grandchildren: 1963.

Birthday party, Gue Shee Lee and extended family, Santa Cruz: Circa 1964.

CHINATOWN DREAMS

Gue Shee Lee with some of her grandchildren, Santa Cruz: 1965.

Gue Shee Lee with grandchildren, baby Karin Yien and Patti Lee: 1965.

Sergeant Henry Chin, Vietnam War Veteran, at Santa Cruz Wharf: Circa 1964.

Kim Wong and George Ow visiting their aunt at Dung Woo, their home village in southern China: 1988.

Entrance to Dung Woo village in China: 1988.

Rose Lee Wong, Priscilla Lee and Gue Shee Lee at age 84: 1984.

Rose Lee Wong and Kim Wong, Santa Cruz: 1996.

Kim Wong and granddaughter Chelsea: 1996.

George Lee, shooting Miss California photos at
Santa Cruz Beach: 1949.

George Lee at Kodak Processing Plant,
Palo Alto: 1955.

Captions and Commentary on Selected Photographs

George Lee with F-1 Aerial Camera, Pensacola, Florida: 1943.

George Lee, Seaman Second Class, with Graflex, at naval photography school; Pensacola, Florida: 1943.

This is one of several World War II photos depicting George Lee, a small-town Chinatown boy who had graduated from Santa Cruz High School in 1941 and joined the Navy. At that time, Hitler had conquered all of Western Europe except England, and he was concentrating on gobbling up Russia and North Africa. Tojo had stunned America at Pearl Harbor and the rising sun flew over the Philippines, much of Pacific Oceana, the Dutch East Indies, Singapore, much of China and Burma, and was heading for India and Australia. Chinese Americans were very aware of the very brutal way in which their relatives and country folk were being slaughtered by Tojo's soldiers. Uncle George didn't want to have the same thing happening in Santa Cruz.

Uncle George was Chinatown's best, and the Navy took him. It gave him good clothes, got him in great physical shape and fed him more food than he ever had in Chinatown. He loved cameras, and the Navy trained him in photography—so Uncle George got to use those wonderful cameras. The Navy sent him to Idaho, Florida, and to numerous islands in the South Pacific, such as the New Hebrides, New Guinea, Tahiti and Hawai'i. He got to see the wonderful places that fellow Navy man James Michener wrote about in *Tales of the South Pacific*. George became an aerial photographer and took pictures of enemy ships and enemy-held islands. He was an important part of a magnificent winning team. He was proud to be in the Navy and to do his part.

George Lee at Webber's Photo Shop: 1958. Shown with an array of expensive German cameras—just before Japanese cameras entered and dominated the camera market. At first, no one could believe that the Japanese could make cameras that could compete with German and American cameras.

George Lee with Rolleicord: Circa 1941. After graduation from Santa Cruz High School in 1941, George Lee commuted to what is now Hartnell Junior College in Salinas, becoming the first person in the Lee family to attend college.

George Lee with photo enlarger. We think this was taken during his Navy years in the South Pacific. Geoffrey Dunn found this "lost" photo while combing George Lee's estate, going through boxes and boxes with many thousands of photos and negatives.

George Lee taking pictures on a ladder: Later 1940s, after World War II; photo taken by Ed Webber. You could tell Uncle George had a lot of fun doing his job. There were half a dozen independent drug stores in downtown Santa Cruz, like Mock's Drugs and Fountain in the background. Covello & Covello, photographers and Santa Cruz photo archivists, have given their gracious permission for use of this photo, as well as the photo on page 53.

Sung Si Lee, father of George Lee, immigration photo: 1903. He worked in America for over 50 years. During the last 20 years, he was the cook at the Wilder Ranch. On tours of the Wilder Ranch, the docent shows tourists a room next to the kitchen called "the Chinese cook's room." This was my grandfather's room for 20 years.

I remember my grandfather as a tall, thin, old man who slept on a cot and walked very slowly. He dressed heavily, as he was always cold. As a young boy, I would rummage through his things and he would get angry with me for messing up his stuff. I remember that he had a package of Bull Durham tobacco and some rolling papers. He had a few pennies and a thin Mercury-head dime. I remember knowing then that it wasn't much to have. But he was a lucky one. His kids were now growing up and could help him. His less-fortunate buddies got their tobacco by picking through butts on the street and using the tobacco that was left.

My mother was always upbeat and positive about people. The one exception was when Uncle George asked her if she wanted to visit the Wilders, who were in the same nursing home as 100-year-old George Mattison, whom we were all visiting. She said she didn't, which sounded strange to me. Later, I asked her about that and she said that her father had worked for the Wilders for 20 years and when he got old and couldn't work anymore, they didn't give him a pension or anything. Uncle George didn't feel that way. I think he felt that the Wilders had done enough by being decent employers, allowing his father to feed his family for 20 years.

Gue Shee Lee, mother of George Lee, immigration photo: 1922. Sometimes I would overhear my grandmother talking to one of her friends about Angel Island. She made it sound like a terrible and scary place. You even had to take off all of your clothes, etc. I never wanted to go there after hearing her talk about it.

She was able to enter the United States because my grandfather paid for some papers that said that he was a partner in a store in Chinatown San Francisco—thus, a merchant. This was a ruse, but one that got his wife through the discriminatory immigration laws. It is said that the immigration people knew what was happening, too, but that they received $300-per-person bribes to let people in; that was a lot of money when a common wage was $1 per day.

Gue Shee Lee holding baby Young and Wee, Santa Cruz Chinatown: 1931. This picture and the one following, along with those on pages 44 and 73, were taken by George Lee's first- or second-grade teacher, Miss Alice Halsey, of Laurel Elementary School. George Lee and Alice Halsey kept in contact for over 40 years. I thank sensitive and supportive teachers like Alice Halsey who provided us with these priceless photos. The family wouldn't have any photos of this time period otherwise. She also eased the cultural assimilation process and collected the clothes that my mother and her siblings are wearing. They were able to be stylish and warm because of a caring teacher.

Lee Lam Bok: 1941. Lee Lam Bok and his peers worked a lifetime in California without family, providing the very necessary hard-working cheap labor to build Western America: a few years making farmland out of marshes; a few years picking; a few years building walls; a few years in a railroad camp; a few years cooking at a ranch. The robust and hopeful teenager is now an old man stranded in the strange land in which he has lived and labored some 60 years. Most of his peers are dead. A few lucky ones made it back to China a long time ago. Lee Lam Bok is one of the last survivors.

Webber's Photo Shop: 1950s. Uncle George took great pride in making the window and other in-store displays beautiful. He won awards from Kodak and other companies for his displays. This was the era when local, independent businesses were the norm and when businesses were passed down from generation to generation. Even though he was an employee and not family, Uncle George felt great pride in his job and gave 100 percent. He wanted to repay Ed Webber for "taking a chance on hiring Chinese" and he knew he had to be "extra good" for any doubting customers and to pave the way for other Chinese.

George Lee's press pass: 1950s. George Lee had a good relationship with the *Santa Cruz Sentinel*. He delivered newspapers for them as a boy and took hundreds of photos for them as an adult. He got to know people while doing what he loved, taking and developing pictures—and people got to know him. Geno Pini was the Police Chief of Santa Cruz for many years.

Patti Lee with firecrackers. Patti is the daughter of George Lee and Priscilla Wong Lee. This picture was picked up by the AP Wire Services and was shown in newspapers all over the United States.

Santa Cruz Chinatown: Early 1940s. Chinatown is gone—a ghost of a place two short blocks from main street and the police station. Gambling, illegal liquor, opium and "fun girls" are gone, and the sojourners are dead or in old age. A few lucky ones made it back to China; some moved to San Francisco. Times have changed, and the more successful Chinese have homes outside of Chinatown. Almost everyone who lived there or visited is gone, and many of the buildings are abandoned and eerie. Eventually, only the Lee family remains. It is a dream, a memory. But I can feel the spirits of the old-timers anytime I walk from Cooper Street down the alley between the Galleria buildings to the San Lorenzo River. I can pull out the priceless photos that Uncle George took and be back in a flash to the wonderful old world of Chinatown.

Chinatown houses: 1941. A flounder is drying on the top porch of the house to the right.

Moon Lai Bok hanging laundry at Chee Kong Tong Temple: 1941. A piece of home in a foreign land; a meeting place for the working men on Sunday; a place to catch up with friends. Once filled with lively, hardworking young men—all gone now,

except for a few old men living their last days on Earth. Who will send their bones to China?

Yee Hen Bok smoking self-rolled Bull Durham cigarette: 1941. One of the last of the men who came to America in the tens of thousands as hopeful teenagers ready to work and make a success in Gold Mountain. These men had the responsibility of working and sending money back to their villages in southern China so that their mothers, fathers, brothers and sisters would not, literally, starve to death. They dreamed of striking it rich and going back to China in style, but most could not overcome the harsh racism of the time and went back as bones.

Ah Fook and George Ow, Jr.: 1948. I was one of the few children in Chinatown. The old men didn't have families and were good to me. Ah Fook loved fishing at the Santa Cruz Wharf and was a well-known figure there. One of my favorite things was thick, sweetened condensed milk and white bread sandwiches.

Last occupied building in Chinatown; Allan Liu and Jun Lee playing near George Lee's Western Flyer bicycle: 1941. George Lee bought the bike with money earned by delivering *Santa Cruz Sentinel* newspapers. Note the newspaper carrying bags.

Georgina Wong and George Ow, Jr.: Chinatown, 1947. Chinatown and the gardens by the river were full of fruit trees: tasty red and yellow cherry plums, Santa Rosa plums, red and green apple trees, peaches and a giant fig tree. Both Georgina and I would go on to get degrees at San Francisco State College.

Gue Shee Lee harvesting corn beside the San Lorenzo River with grandchildren George Ow, Jr., and David Lee Ow: 1949. The garden lay between Grandma's house and the river. It was full of good growing things to eat. Harvesting corn, squash, beans, etc., was a lot of fun. There was a chicken coop, and every Sunday a chicken would be slaughtered for dinner. Auntie Lu remembers sharing one chicken among nine people during the lean days of the Depression. Sometimes the chicken would get away and fly through the air with its head cut off. Everything would be used, including blood for soup and the tasty feet (an acquired taste). The feathers would be mixed with vinegar and rubbed on the skin as a cure for poison oak.

Rose Lee and Kim Wong: 1941. Young and in love—when you had each other, it didn't matter that the world was going up in flames or that you lived in the poorest part of town.

George Ow, Jr., reading the *Service Cardinal:* 1950. Mother, Emily Lee Ow, is holding newly born Terry and father, George Ow, is reading the Chinese magazine.

George Ow, Jr., and David Lee Ow: 1951. We are all dressed up!

Ronald and Linda Wong in front of grandmother Gue Shee Lee's chicken coop: 1954. Ron and Linda are two of Gue Shee Lee's 17 grandchildren and are the children of Rose Lee Wong and Kim Wong.

Wee Lee with steelhead, Luella Lee holding George Ow, Jr.: 1943. Being the first grandchild on the Lee side, I always had a lot of loving babysitters. Uncle Wee graduated from Santa Cruz High School in 1946, served in the Korean War and had a career as a cook at Fort Ord. Luella graduated from Santa Cruz High in 1950, went to nursing school in San Francisco and accumulated enough Santa Cruz real estate to retire in Kauai.

Young Lee holding steelhead caught in the San Lorenzo River: 1946. This was a fairly prosperous time for the Lee family, as evidenced by the nice bicycles, new Levis and sturdy shirt. Uncle George had savings from the Navy and had a good job at Webber's Photo Shop; the older boys were delivering papers and the older girls were cleaning houses. Uncle Wee and Uncle Young were great fisherman who did their share to feed the family by providing delicious fish from the river and the ocean. In those days, you could go to the wharf and catch as many fish as you wanted. Uncle Young drowned while fishing on the Trinity River in 1948. He was wearing oversized waders that filled with water, and he was swept away by the powerful winter-swollen river.

George Ow with his Hupmobile: 1941. George Ow was sent out of China in 1937 as a 17-year-old. His father wanted him to escape the Japanese War. He adapted quickly to America—aided greatly by George Lee, who befriended him and showed him the ropes—and became a fancy dresser with a car. They would become in-laws when George Ow married George Lee's sister Emily.

George Lee: 1948. Working with Rolleiflex 2.8C at Webber's Photo Shop, Santa Cruz. After World War II, service buddy Ed Webber made a pioneering move and gave Uncle George a job at his photo store on Pacific Avenue. Uncle George was one of the first Chinese to be hired to work "up front" in a retail store not owned by Chinese. He stayed at that job for more than 30 years and became one of the best-known and best-liked people in the downtown Santa Cruz community.

Ed Webber photo of Moon Lai Bok and George Ow, Jr.: 1947. Mr. Webber won a blue ribbon at the Santa Cruz County Fair with this picture.

Chinatown Sunset: 1941. A beautiful sunset—with the technological riches of America bringing electricity and telephone service even to lowly Chinatown. The home villages in China would not get electricity until the 1980s or telephones until the 1990s.

The end of Chinatown—the December 1955 Flood. Jun Lee (left, in hip waders) and George Lee (right) in the floodwaters at Pacific Avenue and Church Street, Santa Cruz. Photo credit: Ed Webber.

Uncle Jun had come home from Lassen College for Christmas break. As he describes the event: "It had been raining heavily and the water level was rising under the houses in Chinatown. This wasn't unusual, and the houses had been built to accommodate flooding at the underfloor level. That night, several Red Cross volunteers came by with soup and the latest information; I believe Alan Holbert was among them. Subsequently, Uncle George arrived and said we had to leave, as the river was cresting. Poa and Arnold left to spend the night with daughter Rosie and son-in-law Kim Wong in their Glenview Avenue house on the Eastside. I joined Uncle George at Webber's Photo Shop, where we worked to help move the stock to higher levels, away from the floodwaters. This was a huge job, since most of the extra stock was in the basement. I saw Sam Leask across the street, caulking the glass doors. I was wearing a pair of Uncle Young's waders and was the only dry one at Webber's that night!

"After doing what we could, we all locked arms to cross Pacific Avenue, which by that time had water up to our knees. Several people were taking pictures that night; someone took a picture of Uncle George with his camera, with the river swirling around him. Another picture I remember was of us sitting on sandbags in front of the door, and there was even one of a Nash Metropolitan which had floated down Pacific Avenue and was hung up on a parking meter.

"I ended up that night sleeping on the floor at the Westside house of one of the men who worked for Webber's. The next morning the water had receded, so we went down to Webber's to help clean up. The scene I remember was walking down to the basement and finding that all of the flash bulbs were hanging from the ceiling, stuck there with gluelike mud from the flood holding them in place.

"When we were able to get back to Chinatown, we found that the flood level had reached the top drawer of the dressers, having wicked up the bed spreads. What a mess that was! We hosed down the floors and shoveled out the mud—and life went on. The Red Cross came down and took us to Penney's for some clothes. I ended up with a new turquoise nylon jacket, which came in very handy in snow-covered Susanville when I returned to college a few days later."

Jun Lee went on to graduate from Lassen College, and later got two degrees at San Jose State College, was mayor of Scotts Valley, and became a real estate magnate. This photo is courtesy of Covello & Covello, photographers and Santa Cruz photo archivists.

Tonkinese selling grass skirts, Espiritu Santo, New Hebrides Islands: 1944. Just like Bloody Mary in *South Pacific*.

George Lee's quarters at Espiritu Santo, New Hebrides Islands: 1944. With pictures of Priscilla Wong, his sweetheart, and Emily Lee, his sister, to remind him of home.

Earl Towne with George Lee, Santa Cruz: 1945. Earl Towne and George Lee were Santa Cruz High buddies. They were going to join the Navy together, but Earl was engrossed in working on his car and missed the appointment. He later joined the Army and was sent to fight in Europe. Uncle George and Earl kept in touch by writing letters. Then Earl's letters stopped coming and Uncle George heard that he was killed in the Battle of the Bulge, when Hitler made his last-gasp offensive and took the Allies by surprise. When Earl showed up to visit him in Santa Cruz after the war, Uncle George thought it was a ghost. Earl had been shot in the stomach and captured. He survived because the Germans felt that he looked like them, so blond and Aryan-looking. They asked him repeatedly why he wasn't on their side. Earl looked so good because he had spent the last few months at the Casa Del Rey, which was used by recuperating wounded servicemen.

YWCA, Honolulu, Hawai'i: 1944. Honolulu citizens made Chinese servicemen feel especially welcome because during World War I, Chinese Hawai'ian troops were treated badly away from home. Uncle George beams when he talks about staying at the Royal Hawaiian Hotel for 25 cents a night while on R&R. Can you imagine being young and healthy, a part of a victorious Navy celebrating at Waikiki Beach when there was only the old white Moana Hotel and the bright pink Royal Hawaiian? Uncle George was amazed that one could walk so far out in the warm water.

R&R, Honolulu, Hawai'i, with Seventh Division troopers just back from Kwajalein: 1944. The Seventh Division troopers had stories of Chinese buddies being mistakenly shot as Japanese because they spoke only broken English.

George Ow returned from WWII: 1945. When Chinese Filipinos saw my father as part of the liberating American forces, he was looked upon as a conquering hero.

George Lee, Aviation Photographer's Mate, Second Class, with Leica; Philadelphia Naval Yard: 1950. He is shown well dressed in his Navy whites, with his wonderful Leica camera. Uncle George was called up when the Korean War started. By this time he had a wife and daughter, but he went willingly to do his duty.

Frazier Lewis House, East Cliff Drive, Santa Cruz: Circa 1910. Frazier Lewis was the son of Patty Reed, the brave little girl who virtually walked across the Western United States as part of the Donner Party. The childless Lewis family befriended George Lee and gave him famous Frazier Lewis candy and his first camera. They had him take a picture of Patty Reed's doll—the one she carried on the trip—at the house. Uncle George said that he lost touch with them when he went into the Navy; when he returned, they had all died. The house is now owned by writers James D. Houston and Jeanne Wakatsuki Houston. James Houston does his writing up in the cupola.

David Lee Ow with Oscar Presley: Circa 1948. Chinatown was a safe (accepted) place where people of color could live in Santa Cruz.

Ernest Otto at George Lee's wedding dinner: 1949. Ernest Otto wrote for the *Santa Cruz Sentinel* and other newspapers for over 50 years. He was a friend to the Chinese and included us in his stories.

Miss California Pageant, Santa Cruz Beach Boardwalk: Circa 1950. This was a big deal and brought a lot of excitement to Santa Cruz.

Rock Cod Lines, Santa Cruz Wharf: 1941. There were strong ties between the Chinese and Italian fishing families. Gilda Stagnaro was a great friend of George Lee and helped welcome George Ow to Santa Cruz High School when he arrived from China. Gilda still welcomes George Ow 60-plus years later, as he lunches regularly at her restaurant on the wharf.

Twin Lakes Beach, Santa Cruz: 1950. Pilings from the old trolley line that ran between Santa Cruz and Capitola are exposed.

Supreme Court Building, Washington, D.C.: 1951. George Lee was stationed in Philadelphia during the Korean War and was able to visit our nation's capital and other nearby cities.

Hoy Lew at age 92. Portrait session, Cabrillo College: Circa 1990. George Lee was teaching a photography class and invited his striking and long-lived friend to pose. Hoy Lew had many opportunities to buy farms and ranches during the 1920s and 1930s, when prices had hit rock bottom. He couldn't buy—even though he had the money—because it was against the law for Chinese not born in America to own land. Hoy Lew could have been a local land baron and a rich man, had he been afforded equal protection under the law.

Lam Pon Family, just before returning to China: 1930. Left to right: George (who would return to the United States in 1937 as George Ow), Mrs. Lam Pon (Lam Ow High), Lam Pon, Anna Lam (who had just graduated from Santa Cruz High School, Class of 1930). It was written in the *Santa Cruz Sentinel* that Anna Lam and Sue Chin, classmates in the graduating class of June 1930, were the first Chinese students to graduate from Santa Cruz High School.

Lam Pon lived through the Japanese invasion and World War II, the civil war between the Communists and Nationalists, the victory of the Communists in 1949 and the Cultural Revolution. During World War II, Lam Pon fled back to the village and Japanese soldiers sacked his Canton house, throwing all of the furniture out of the house, even from the second and third floors. There was starvation during those war years, and I met a woman in the village during a 1990 visit (Lam Pon's sister-in-law), whose two children starved to death during this time. During the Communist takeover and the Cultural Revolution, Lam Pon was fingered by this same sister-in-law as a capitalist who had been to America.

While in the United States, Lam Pon was a prosperous businessman who had helped start an apple dryer business, the Sanitary Café and a small bank. His younger brother, Lam Sing, went into the grocery business and operated the Canton Market on Pacific Avenue and Cathcart Street for many years. Both brothers and their children became owners of many parcels of land after the rescinding, in 1943, of the 1882 anti-Chinese laws (which, among other things, prohibited Chinese not born in the United States from owning land). Lam Pon had returned to China in 1930, partly because the laws and society in America kept him from fully enjoying his business success.

Anna Lam Liu with sons, Allan and Donny, at their house on Younglove Avenue, Santa Cruz: 1948. Anna Liu worked hard and saved her money to buy a house out of the confines of Chinatown. Anna and her children came to the United States in 1940. Her husband George Liu could not enter and had to wait out the war and its aftermath (1940–1949) in China before being reunited with his family.

George Liu at Coit Tower, San Francisco: 1949. Everyone was happy when Uncle George was able to come over from China. He was from Australia.

Drying out after the December 1955 Flood: 1956. There were a couple of feet of mud inside the house. Downtown was flooded, too. Gue Shee Lee had already experienced flood and the resulting famine in China. Then she came to America to find her Chinatown next to an unpredictable river.

Gambling Houses being demolished: 1956. The Palomar Hotel and the old jail (now the Museum of Art and History) can be seen in the background.

Chinese passport with photo, Wong Family—Lucille, Joong Seu, Priscilla: 1939. Japan has captured much of coastal China and is bearing down on Canton. The Chinese know about Nanking and how Japanese troops have been treating civilians in captured areas. It is very difficult and costly to get a Chinese passport and almost impossible to get admission to the United States. But if you don't get out, you are probably going to end up dead or deadly brutalized. The dazed look on all three faces reflects this.

The situation reminds me of Ingrid Bergman escaping the Nazis in Casablanca, or Danton escaping the guillotine in *A Tale of Two Cities,* or of the ships filled with Jewish refugees trying to escape Hitler's ovens that were turned back in sight of New York by America.

With lots of grit and determination, some connections and payoff money, some luck and ingenuity, Joong Seu and daughters, Lucille and Priscilla, leave their Toisan area village with a passport. They go to Macao, then Hong Kong. A visa is obtained for a visit to America. They have somehow won the biggest lottery, that of life. Oldest sister, Jin Yu, stays in British-held Hong Kong to finish high school. They believed Japan would not be crazy enough to attack the British Empire. But Japan does attack and Jin Yu has to fend for herself. She somehow gets back to the home village. The family would not see her again until 1980, over 40 years later.

George Wong, immigration photo: 1924. George Wong was the father of Priscilla Wong, Georgina Wong, Lucille Wong and Jin Yu Wong. He was a business partner of Malio J. Stagnaro, great-uncle of *Chinatown Dreams* editor Geoffrey Dunn.

Margery Woo, high school graduation photo, China: Late 1930s. Margery Woo was a Santa Cruz girl who was a second cousin of Uncle George. She left Chinatown and was brought to China as a young girl in the 1920s. In China, she lived a privileged life—even among war, famine and disorder—because her father had done well in America and had money. During World War II, her family fled to the interior and she studied piano. She returned to the United States after World War II and worked for the United States Mint in San Francisco for many years. I remember seeing her as a beautiful and sophisticated young woman visiting Chinatown in the late 1940s and then at a family gathering in the 1970s. Uncle George would keep in contact with her and visit her in San Francisco.

One day in the 1990s, she jumped off a building in Chinatown and died. Uncle George was her executor. To his surprise, she had left a goodly amount of money to her old school and old teachers in China and some charities in America. She had a low-level, low-paying job at the Mint, but she lived frugally and saved every penny. Uncle George tracked down the old teachers who were living—one was 95 years old—and the families of the deceased teachers. It was a heaven-sent windfall for them.

Joong Seu Wong with daughters Priscilla, Lucille and Georgina, Santa Cruz: 1948. Relaxed, safe, fattened-up and with a new America-born daughter. One might not be the first hired or be able to buy a house in many neighborhoods, but America was heaven compared to China. Contrast this picture with the Wong family Chinese passport photo on page 100.

Rose Lee with George Ow, Jr.: 1943. I felt that I had a legion of loving relatives to take care of me in Chinatown.

Kim Wong and Rose Lee Wong: 1948. Uncle Hong worked all kinds of jobs, finally landing a good union job as a retail clerk. Auntie Rose raised two children and worked for over 30 years in the Santa Cruz canneries. She and Auntie Priscilla and their co-workers were in the line when the last Santa Cruz canning operation closed down—the Monterey Mushroom line at the Seabright Cannery.

George Lee and Priscilla Wong: 1947. The prosperity after World War II and the ability to earn decent money are reflected in their sharp clothing and confident smiles. Uncle George and Auntie Priscilla were both working on Pacific Avenue at this time. Uncle George was working at Webber's Photo Shop and Auntie Priscilla was working at National Dollar Store—a chain of stores that was a cross between a small department store and a 5-and-10-cent variety store. National Dollar Store was possibly the largest Chinese-American business in the country, with branches in many California and Arizona cities.

Santa Cruz Parade with George Liu (center) standing behind (left to right) his sons, Donny and Allan, with Georgina Wong and Priscilla Wong Lee, in front of Webber's Photo Shop, Santa Cruz: 1949.

George Ow with David Lee Ow: 1947. Dad was always a sharp dresser and always wore slacks, a nice shirt and a tie beneath his grocer-butcher's smock.

George Ow with George, Jr., and David at Santa Cruz Boardwalk: Circa 1948. Cotton candy and French fries were special Boardwalk treats. I remember how warm and tasty the French fries were and how expensive they seemed at 20 cents a bag—two whole dimes.

George Ow with David and George, Jr., at Santa Cruz Beach: 1950. Going to the beach was rare and exciting. The water was cold and the waves were both exhilarating and terrifying. I wished that I had a regular bathing suit and not just my underwear.

Gary Ow, George Ow and Bing Yue Ow in front of the Gary Brothers Market in Gadsden Arizona: Early 1950s. George Ow entered the United States in 1937 as Bing Yue Ow's son. Actually, Bing Yue Ow was the brother of his adoptive mother, but those were the papers that were available. You had to be ingenious and devious to get around discriminatory and racist laws.

Chinatown Dinner: 1949. Seated from left: George Ow, Jr., mugging with turkey drumstick, Emily Lee Ow, George Ow, Wee Lee, David Ow, Rose Lee Wong. Standing from left: Georgina Wong, Jun Lee, Kim Wong holding Linda Wong, Priscilla Wong Lee, Luella Lee, Gue Shee Lee.

Ow and Lam-Liu Families, Chinatown Santa Cruz: 1950. Back row: Emily Lee Ow holding baby Richard Ow, George Ow holding young Terry Ow, Mrs. Lam Pon (Lam Ow High), Anna Lam Liu holding young Nancy Liu. Front row: David Ow, George Ow, Jr., Don Liu, Allan Liu.

Sisters Priscilla Wong Lee and Georgina Wong at Christmas: 1950. Becoming Americans.

Extended family picture taken at Santa Cruz City Hall with ivy-covered old Carnegie Library in background: 1949. Back row: George Lee, Kim Wong, Gue Shee Lee, Emily Lee Ow, Luella Lee, Rose Lee Wong. Front row; Priscilla Wong Lee with hands on her sister, Georgina Wong, Jun Lee, Allan Liu, Don Liu, David Ow, George Ow, Jr.

Ow-Lam-Liu Families, Monterey, California: 1954. Standing, left to right: Anna Lam Liu, Mary Ow being held by George Ow, Emily Ow holding Tommy Ow, George Ow, Jr. with hands on Nancy Liu, Don Liu and Allan Liu with David Ow in front of them and Richard Ow in front of David Ow. Terry Ow stands in front of Mary. Seated is Anna Lam Liu's mother, Mrs. Lam Pon, holding baby Jeannee Ow. We had a nice big television and a nice set of *Encyclopedia Americana*. I read those encyclopedias for fun.

Family of George and Joong Seu Wong, Santa Cruz: 1959. Standing: George Wong flanked by sons-in-law Wah Wong, in glasses (husband of Lucille Wong and father of Terry Wong), and George Lee, in tie (and living up to his Chinese nickname of *Go,* meaning "tall"). Sitting (left to right): Patti Lee next to mother, Priscilla Wong Lee, Georgina Wong, Joong Seu Wong, Lucille Wong with daughter, Terry.

Gue Shee Lee and Grandchildren: 1963. Back row, left to right: George Ow, Jr., Terry Ow, Judy Willis Ow, David Ow holding Karin Yien, Linda Wong, Mary Ow. Front row, standing: Ron Wong, Richard Ow, Tommy Ow, Gue Shee Lee holding Suzi Yien, Jeannee Ow, Patti Lee. Down in front: Larry Yien and Loni Yien. Uncle Bob Yien was a hard-working and successful dentist who graduated from UC San Francisco, and Luella Lee Yien was a nurse. They built a big, beautiful house below DeLaveaga Golf Course, where this picture was taken.

Birthday party, Santa Cruz: Circa 1964. Gue Shee Lee and extended family. Sitting, left to right: Judy Willis Ow with daughter, baby Karen Ow. George Ow, Gue Shee Lee holding Suzi Yien, Jeannee Ow, Loni Yien with hand on chin, Wee Lee. Standing, left to right: Luella Lee Yien, Jun Lee, Linda Wong, Mary Ow, Emily Lee Ow, George Lee holding Larry Yien, Richard Ow, Rose Lee Wong. Extreme back row, left to right: George Ow, Jr., Tommy Ow, Terry Ow, Ron Wong, David Ow.

Gue Shee Lee with some of her grandchildren, Santa Cruz: 1965. Left to right: Larry Yien, Jeannee Ow, Mary Ow, Gue Shee Lee with Karin Yien, Loni Yien, Patti Lee.

Gue Shee Lee with grandchildren, baby Karin Yien and Patti Lee: 1965. Karin would later graduate from Mills College and Harvard Medical School and Patti would graduate from the University of California at Santa Barbara.

Sergeant Henry Chin at Santa Cruz Wharf: Circa 1964. Uncle George said that Henry Chin (Class of 1947, Santa Cruz High School) was the first Chinese to be invited into the Hi Tow Tong, the boy's honor society at Santa Cruz High School. He also played sports and was an outgoing, gregarious person. He loved fishing on the wharf with Robert "Big Boy" Stagnaro, Wee Lee and Young Lee. During the 1968 Tet Offensive in Vietnam, the Vietcong and North Vietnamese Regulars surrounded Henry's compound. The only food he had was dried noodles that Uncle George had mailed him in a care package. Uncle George comes through once again!

Henry Chin had served 25 years in the Air Force when he felt that something was wrong with his health. The Air Force doctors couldn't find anything wrong, so his superiors thought he was malingering. Less than 30 days after noting that something was wrong, Henry died. They found out he had cancer.

Kim Wong and George Ow visiting their aunt at Dung Woo, their home village in southern China: 1988. This was their first visit in over 45 years and they were greeted as though they had just left for America a month earlier. They both had lived in this house as boys.

This was the Lam Village (also Lum or Lim, depending on the dialect). In Chinese calligraphy, it is two trees, perhaps translated as "Forest" in English. The name was *Dung Woo,* or "East Lake." Across the marshy pond/field was another Lam Village called *See Woo,* or "West Lake." My father remembers it as a long walk through rural fields from the market at Toisan. Charlie Lee, a villager who sold melons, remembered walking

with melons bundled and hung on poles. He would walk for hours in the predawn to get to market. The worst thing was if he didn't sell any and would have to carry them back home.

When I visited the village with my father in 1990, it was a short ride from the center of Toisan. When I revisited in 1997, there had been tremendous growth. Toisan was expanding outward in all directions and was ready to engulf Dung Woo. Some village land toward the main road had already been sold for commercial and industrial uses and it was only a question of time before the rice fields would be built over.

Entrance to Dung Woo village in China: 1988. The walls and fortress-like entrance were useful in defending the village during bad times. The village had many empty houses. Many families had gone to America or Canton or Toisan. Farming, while a good traditional life, was hard work and young people wanted something better and a more exciting life. My father noticed, during his first visit in the early 1980s, that there was a tile floor versus the dirt floor that he remembered, and there were bags of rice in the storage loft where he and his grandmother slept. The next time, there was electricity, then television, then a telephone actually in the house. What great changes.

Kim Wong and Rose Lee Wong, Santa Cruz: 1996. Uncle Hong (Kim Wong) died in 1996.

George Lee, shooting Miss California photos at Santa Cruz Beach: 1949. A photo lover with top-of-the-line cameras, shooting beautiful women on a sunny day at the old Santa Cruz Wharf. What more could one want?

George Lee at Kodak Processing Plant, Palo Alto: 1955. No matter where he went, Uncle George made friends. He was a great ambassador for Webber's Photo Shop, our family and Chinese people in general. He was the unofficial "mayor of Chinatown."

Contributors

Geoffrey Dunn is an award-winning journalist, filmmaker and historian and has written extensively about documentary film and photography. He is the author of *Santa Cruz Is in the Heart* and co-director of several documentary films for public television, including *Dollar a Day, 10¢ a Dance: A Historic Portrait of Filipino Farm Workers in America*; *Chinese Gold* (based on the book by Sandy Lydon); *Mi Vida: The Three Worlds of Maria Gutierrez*; and *Miss…or Myth?* He also wrote the original screenplay for the feature film *Maddalena Z.* The winner of a 2002 Gail Rich Award for artistic contributions to Santa Cruz County, Dunn currently serves as a Lecturer in the Community Studies Department of the University of California, Santa Cruz, and as Executive Director of Community Television of Santa Cruz County.

Lisa Liu Grady is a freelance writer with nonfiction publications in the *San Francisco Chronicle* and *San Francisco Examiner*. She holds an M.F.A. in creative writing from Mills College and is currently at work on her first book, a memoir that combines her former career as a navigating officer onboard commercial oil tankers in the United States Merchant Marine with her family's rich legacy in marine transportation that now stretches three generations. She lives in Emerald Hills, California, with her husband, Jim. Of her relationship to George Lee, she says: "I don't think that there is any easy way to explain our relationship, other than the fact that he is the brother-in-law of George Ow, Sr., my grandmother Anna's brother. I always called him 'Uncle George' and remember him not only as the chronicler of our family through photographs but also as a very kind and generous person who sent us delicious mooncakes through the mail during the August Moon Festival."

Tony Hill was born and raised in Harlem, New York City. In 1957, he was one of the first school children bused to achieve "integration" as a result of the historic Supreme Court decision in *Brown v. Board of Education* three years earlier. He later attended City College of New York, pursuing a career in Industrial Psychology. In 1972, he left New York City and moved to California, where he went to work at a residential treatment center for emotionally disturbed adolescents. In the early 1980s, Hill started the local television station KRUZ for Group W Cable. Recently, he founded Access Unlimited, specializing in Organizational Development, and currently serves as the creator of "Welcoming Diversity" workshops and seminars. Hill says of his diversity efforts: "I'm passionate about my work and want to challenge us to look more closely at ourselves and others, so that together, we may bring about positive change, build self-esteem and bridge differences in our community."

James D. Houston is the author of a dozen works of fiction and nonfiction exploring the cultures and histories of the western United States and the Asia/Pacific region. His novel, *The Last Paradise,* set in Hawai'i, received a 1999 American Book Award. With his wife, Jeanne Wakatsuki Houston, he co-authored *Farewell to Manzanar,* now a standard work in schools and colleges across the country. His recent novel, *Snow Mountain Passage,* based on the Reed family's experiences during 1846–1847, was named one of the year's best books by the *Los Angeles Times* and the *Washington Post*. It was inspired by the history of the Frazier Lewis House, where Patty Reed Lewis spent the last years of her long life, and where the Houstons have lived since 1962.

Sandy Lydon is Historian Emeritus at Cabrillo College, Aptos, California, where he has taught since 1968. A graduate of the East-West Center, Honolulu, his teaching has focused on East Asian and Asian American History. His book, *Chinese Gold: The Chinese in the Monterey Bay Region*, was awarded the Book of the Year from the Association for Asian-American Studies and served as the basis for a museum exhibit and film. He has since published *The Japanese in the Monterey Bay Region: A Brief History* as well as being the co-author of a book on California's Coast Redwoods. Lydon describes himself as a "retroactive affirmative action officer....I'm researching the stories of those who were left out of the histories of the Monterey Bay Region and weaving them back into the fabric of this place."

Morton Marcus was born in New York City in 1936, but has lived in Santa Cruz, California, since 1968. He has published nine volumes of poetry and one novel, including *The Santa Cruz Mountain Poems*, *Pages from a Scrapbook of Immigrants*, *When People Could Fly*, *Moments Without Names: New & Selected Prose Poems* and *Shouting Down the Silence*. Marcus has had more than 400 poems published in literary journals, and his work has been selected to appear in over 75 anthologies in the United States, Europe and Australia. A film critic as well as poet, he taught English and film at Cabrillo College for thirty years, until his retirement in 1998, and currently he co-hosts a poetry radio show and a television film review program. In 1999, he was named Santa Cruz County "Artist of the Year."

Mark Stuart Ong is a partner in Side By Side Studios, San Francisco. He has been a book designer for more than twenty-five years, and has designed books in every genre from scholarly books to color art books. His designs have won multiple awards from Bookbuilders West and The Association of American University Presses.

George Ow, Jr., is the son of George Ow and Emily Lee Ow, and the grandson of Sung Si Lee and Gue Shee Lee, and of Lam Pon and Lam Ow High. He was born in Santa Cruz, California, January 3, 1943, and lived his early years in the Santa Cruz Chinatown with his grandmother Lee's family and the last of the old Chinese bachelor pioneers. A graduate of Monterey High School, Monterey Peninsula College and San Francisco State College, Ow received his M.B.A. from the University of California, Los Angeles. He also served as an officer in the United States Army from 1967 to 1970. Currently a Santa Cruz businessman, land developer and bodyboarder, he says: "I was born at the right time and was able to reach high because I could stand on the ready shoulders of those who came before me."